Outsmarting
ANGER

7 Strategies for Defusing Our Most Dangerous Emotion

JOSEPH SHRAND, MD

with Leigh Devine, MS

Harvard Health Publications
HARVARD MEDICAL SCHOOL
Trusted advice for a healthier life

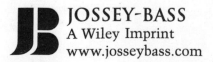

JOSSEY-BASS
A Wiley Imprint
www.josseybass.com

Cover concept: Galen Shrand; cover photographer: Carol Shrand; cover Photoshop: Jason Shrand; cover model: Becca Shrand; book illustrations by Sophia T. Shrand

Published by Jossey-Bass
A Wiley Imprint
One Montgomery Street, Suite 1200, San Francisco, CA 94104-4594—www.josseybass.com

Jossey-Bass books and products are available through most bookstores. To contact Jossey-Bass directly call our Customer Care Department within the U.S. at 800-956-7739, outside the U.S. at 317-572-3986, or fax 317-572-4002.

Wiley publishes in a variety of print and electronic formats and by print-on-demand. Some material included with standard print verfsions of this book may not be included in e-books or in print-on-demand. If this book refers to media such as a CD or DVD that is not included in the version you purchased, you may download this material at http://booksupport.wiley.com. For more information about Wiley products, visit www.wiley.com.

Library of Congress Cataloging-in-Publication Data
Shrand, Joseph, date.
   Outsmarting anger : 7 strategies for defusing our most dangerous emotion / Joseph Shrand, MD, with Leigh Devine, MS. – First edition.
       pages cm
   Includes bibliographical references and index.
   ISBN 978-1-118-13548-8 (cloth); ISBN 978-1-118-22527-1 (ebk.); ISBN 978-1-118-23875-2 (ebk.); ISBN 978-1-118-26337-2 (ebk.)
   1. Anger.   2. Anger–Treatment.   I. Devine, Leigh, date.   II. Title.
   RC569.5.A53S57 2013
   152.4'7–dc23

                              2012048731

Printed in the United States of America
FIRST EDITION
HB Printing   10 9 8 7 6 5 4 3 2 1

Contents

Preface

A few years ago, I started writing a book about the power of respect. In my career as a psychiatrist and throughout my life, I'd observed that when people acted with respect toward one another, feelings of anxiety and anger seemed to diminish. Inspired by this notion, I wrote a nearly complete book before realizing I had no idea how to publish one. So off I went to a seminar offered by Harvard Health Publications on how to publish your book. While there I met some remarkable people, listened to their stories, and shared my ideas.

The day after the seminar was over, I received an email from Dr. Julie Silver, who is the chief editor of books at Harvard Health Publications. To my astonishment, she liked my ideas and asked me if I would consider writing a book with them. Thinking as an editor, she told me that respect might not be compelling enough to grab readers' attention. But anger—now there is a topic everyone can relate to. Anger is exciting, dangerous, mysterious, and primal. It implies a seething, perilous potential for threat and taps in to our deep human desires. Anger is daunting and forbidding and all too pervasive in our modern-day world. Take my idea about the untapped power of respect, suggested Julie, and explore it through the lens of anger.

So I have.

In my profession as a psychiatrist, I have been impressed by how often a patient had become angry to the point of seeming out of touch with reality. When a brain gets to this point, bad things usually happen. But if you confront someone about his anger, he may get even angrier. This direct approach has never worked. And asking him to control his anger, to manage his anger, can also be like putting match to tinder and igniting fury.

But what if, instead of telling someone to manage his anger, we helped do it for him? What if we could actually use our own brain to calm the angry brain of another person? What if we could use our thinking brain to redirect our feeling brain?

One of the most remarkable human abilities we have is one we hardly know how to access. Each of us is inherently able to decrease someone else's anger. This book is not just about anger management. It is about using your brain to outsmart anger in someone else's brain.

Acknowledgments

I acknowledge the following people for helping make this book a reality:

Julie Silver, MD, chief editor of books at Harvard Health Publications, who conceived the idea for this project and assembled the author team. We thank you for your tireless patience and advocacy.

Tony Komaroff, MD, editor in chief of Harvard Health Publications. We appreciate your passion for bringing medical information that is practical, accessible, and accurate to the public.

Linda Konner, our literary agent. Your ability to shape a project and bring all parties to the table is unparalleled.

Liz Neporent, our mutual supportive friend and book-writing champion.

Kate Bradford, our wonderful Jossey-Bass editor, who helped guide us through the writing process and made our pages all the better for it.

The many people at Jossey-Bass, such as Nana Twumasi and Carol Hartland, who kept the production process flowing, and Michele Jones, my copyeditor, whose attention to detail (without *too* much nagging) helped make the book crystal clear.

My friend and writer Leigh Devine who kept the blinkers on me when I would stray, and never got angry with me even once.

My wife and vitamin C, Carol Shrand, who made writing a book on anger about as anger free as it could be. Her sense of humor, laser-like ability to help me clarify even the most dense neuroscience, and ability to enhance my oxytocin are without parallel. I especially thank my kids, Sophie, Jason, Galen, and Becca Mai, who have always proven that a respected child is a valued child and that a child who feels valuable is one step closer to success. Each of them is remarkably successful, of which I am eternally proud.

Christopher Sarson, the creator and executive producer of *Zoom*, who has been my ZoomPapa for forty years. Christopher inspired me to begin the exploration of respect, a journey that led to the heart of this book. His work with Roots of Empathy continues to have an impact. But more than anyone I know, he has dedicated his career to shining a light on the need to see children for who they are and not just for who we wish they were.

Heather Caldera, my nurse manager and long, fast friend who helped me put into practice the power of respect with adolescents struggling with psychiatric conditions, addictions, or both.

Russell Haddleton, Esq., whose friendship and valuable insights from the universe of law helped hone and sharpen the positions in this book. Russ has been a stalwart supporter of my family and myself, and as a friend of my late father has adopted me as his own son.

My brother from another mother, Jim Quine, whose Mensa-like intelligence confirms that he is indeed from the deep end of the gene pool.

A myriad of thinkers and innovators, theorists, and practitioners in fields ranging from sociobiology to psychology to theology, from the neurosciences, economics, and the humanities, providing the opportunity to synthesize their discoveries into the strategies of this book.

Finally, the many scientists, researchers, colleagues, and patients who contributed to the wealth of information in this book, enabling us at long last to use our modern brain to outsmart anger.

Introduction

Put down the chair!" the nurse shrieked, as Dan, a very large psychotic patient, raised the piece of furniture in the air, intent on smashing it over her head. Staff members were already running toward them, ready to put him in restraints. Dan's face was red with the flow of adrenaline, and he was breathing fast and heavy with rage. Just then, a doctor walked calmly into the hallway. "Hey Dan," he said, "Want a cup of coffee?" They all stared for a moment. The doctor said, "Decaf OK?" Dan smiled, lowered the chair, and asked, "With cream?" They both went down to the kitchen for a cup of Joe.

This is a true story, and Dan was my patient. People wondered how I was able to calm Dan's anger within seconds. I, too, have given a lot of thought to this situation and thousands of others that might have turned explosive and even catastrophic but for a calm and respectful intervention. In this short exchange with Dan, I reminded him of his value by approaching him calmly, trustingly, and with empathy for his very visible discomfort. I didn't treat him like a patient. I didn't treat him like someone who had lost control. I treated him with respect. Although it seems remarkably simple, respect extinguished Dan's anger.

We all have the ability to outsmart anger, in others and in ourselves.

An adolescent patient had been in my program for ten days, recovering from a serious heroin addiction. Over that time, she had learned a lot about the impact of drugs on her brain, and the impact of her drugs on other people's brains, such as her parents'. Heroin had a

1

significant hold on her, but she was desperate to be sober. She knew in her heart that she needed longer-term care, but I had told her that addiction doesn't happen in the heart; it happens in the brain.

When her parents told her she could not go home but had to go to further treatment for three months, she lost it and became enraged. Her parents quickly activated their anger response in return, flaring at her that she needed help and would do as she was told. The girl became even more furious and told them she hated them. She resented their power over her, suspected they just wanted to get rid of her, and began screaming and threatening to run away.

She ran out of my office and through the common room, overturning chairs as she went. Her destination, however, was not the door but the relaxation room where kids can go to do just that. Even as staff responded, she found her way to the beanbag chair and threw herself onto it. Still fuming, she began to redirect herself. As she told me later, she had thought her over-the-top anger was in response to her parents' refusal to take her home. But as she became more honest with herself, she began to recognize that she was really angry about not being able to get the stash of dope she had hidden in her room under her bed. She was angry about the power her parents had to send her away, but realized that all they wanted was to try to take away the power that heroin had over her. She had been suspicious that they didn't love her and were abandoning her, and thought that if she didn't mean anything to them, they might as well just let her use dope.

But as she sat in the beanbag chair, flailing her legs and punching the bag, she remembered their faces as they told her she had to go for more care: they were not angry, but sad, somewhat peaceful, and hopeful that she could get better. They had been interested in what she was going through; they cared for her, loved her, valued her. They didn't get angry until she had become angry. And she began to recognize what she had put them through with her addiction.

When she next spoke with her parents, it was with love and the determination to reconnect. She wanted to go home, but wanted to stay home sober. Echoing what she had heard me tell her about an event with my own child years before, she told her parents that she had stopped being mad at them but had never stopped loving them. Together they cried and hugged one another as she thanked them for having the trust in her to get clean. She had outsmarted her anger, and went for further care.

Anger, often called "the fire inside," is one of our most powerful and primal human emotions, as much a part of us as fear and love. It has traveled with us for millennia, sometimes as a weapon and sometimes as a tool. Anger has been used destructively to annihilate neighbors, and productively to protest social injustice. Anger has helped us survive by warding off threats and aggression from others. It is a fire inside designed to have an impact on the outside.

But in the modern world, anger—in all its subtle forms, from frustration to fury—often gets in the way of our success in business, relationships, and everyday social discourse. Because anger, with roots deep in the brain's limbic system, can be so insidious and so intense, people often feel as though they can't control it.

Advances in MRI brain research increasingly suggest the exact opposite. In fact, studies are showing that the brain itself is equipped to buffer and temper the anger response. Recently, University of Wyoming scientists showed that subjects who had first been primed to feel hostility were better able to control anger reactions when armed with "forgiveness" techniques. Their 2010 study, published in the *Journal of Personality and Social Psychology*, suggests that even as the human body gets ready to spring into action, the human mind can also be trained to temper or defuse those actions. Our anger can be transformed into much more productive power. Just as the relatively recent explosion of civilization was profoundly influenced by the taming of fire, the last few million years have resulted in the evolution of a relatively new part of our brain with the potential to tame the fire of anger inside us all.

In *Outsmarting Anger*, we will look at the powerful and primitive origins of anger. You will learn what happens inside the brain when anger begins to bubble and boil, and read about all of the built-in mechanisms you have to counteract its dark forces. Next, I offer seven innovative yet remarkably uncomplicated strategies that anyone can master to help defuse this most dangerous emotion and transform our powerful anger impulses into positive, success-oriented actions. These brain-based techniques will show you how to recognize the many forms of anger you generate, and how to tap in to your brain's very own anger management zone—the prefrontal cortex, or PFC. Although you may not be dealing with addiction, you can learn, as my adolescent female patient did, how to identify why you are angry and then do something about it.

But this is not just another anger management book.

Instead, I will also show you how to use these techniques to transform the anger of *others*, just as I did with Dan, and just as the young girl did with her parents. When you think about it, it is not always *your* anger that gets in the way of your success, but very often the anger of *others* that gets in the way of your success. When we learn to recognize and defuse the anger response of any individual, we improve our chances for success in every aspect of life, ultimately enabling all of us to be more successful. I see this happen every day.

The first strategy discussed in the book, Recognize Rage, shows how to challenge anger by first identifying it. Anger is a powerful feeling, often very uncomfortable both for the person experiencing it and for the person subjected to it. Like pain, it is telling us something useful—but only if we are listening to it. I will show you how and why it is important to "ascertain" your anger, and offer exercises and tips to help you master this technique.

The following strategies, Envision Envy and Sense Suspicion, help you identify two basic triggers that in our modern world commonly breed low levels of anger, such as annoyance or irritation. Envy stems from the idea that you don't have enough and that someone else has more, placing you at a potential survival disadvantage. Sounds simple, right? But at its root, envy stems from one's own self-image—the lower the self-esteem, the more envy.

The flip side of envy is suspicion, and it is every bit as primal. Suspicion originates with the fear that someone will take what's yours—or what should be yours—and leave you out in the cold. If you have ever felt your anxiety rising when standing in a disorganized line to buy a sandwich, you are sensing suspicion. This is because our brains are not designed to trust strangers instantly.

These three strategies exercise your ability to recognize and identify basic feeling states, which, as I explain, are "limbic" functions and part of our ancient primal heritage. Because these are indeed part of *our* heritage, it means that if your brain is doing this, everyone's brain is doing this. Armed with this understanding, you are now in a position to begin outsmarting anger and shifting your brain out of these potentially dangerous, instinctive survival responses. The next four strategies begin to shift the locus of brain control—both in your brain and the brains of angry people whom you may encounter—to the more evolutionarily modern part of our brains, the PFC.

The fourth strategy, Promote Peace, begins to calm the angry brains of the people with whom you are interacting—family, friends, associates, strangers. This strategy sends a message to other people that you are not angry yourself and therefore neither a threat nor someone of whom to be envious or suspicious. By promoting peace, you begin to calm the limbic response of another's brain, creating a foundation for the three remaining strategies.

Engage Empathy is the fifth strategy to outsmart anger. Empathy helps you learn to respect the emotional experience of other people, whatever that may be. By zeroing in on where their anger is, you can influence and even take control of various situations. Because we have evolved the same basic brain, we can influence another person's behavior by being able to assess his or her brain activity. A meta-analysis of studies has shown that empathy has a primary home in the brain (within the medial PFC) and is among a family of other cognitive functions that include our ability to infer other people's emotional judgments and their perceptions of their own bodily state, and valuation of other people's behavior. Empathy continues to place our PFC in the driver's seat in terms of our behavior and interactions. We send a clear message to the other person that we are *interested* in what she thinks and feels, in her experience, and want to know more. When a person feels that you are interested in her, she begins to feel valued by you. The next strategy begins the process of exploring the other person's experience and sharing your own.

The sixth strategy to outsmart anger is Communicate Clearly. Language distinguishes us as humans and has evolved globally over tens of thousands of years. When you learn to communicate clearly, you help the person you're speaking with express his thoughts and feelings and become receptive to yours. You have defused his anger, envy, and suspicion, replacing those negative attributes and the threat of combat with the positive ones of empathy, trust, and the potential for cooperation. In short, you have shown the other person respect. These simple actions bring both individuals into what I call "primary PFC mode," a state in which human beings function at their best—whether they're performing on stage or sending spacecraft into orbit.

The final strategy, Trade Thanks, completes the seven strategies to outsmarting anger, firmly establishing our PFC as the influence on our limbic system, rather than the reverse. Trading thanks uses your PFC to stimulate a limbic response in another person. But this limbic response feels great—and why would anyone want to change that? Anger is designed to change the behavior of someone else, but we don't get angry when being thanked because it feels too good. It is when we are not thanked and recognized for our ability that we can get angry. If you've ever noticed a clerk who doesn't say thank you after you've purchased an item, or if you've ever sent a gift to someone and not had it acknowledged, then you have noticed how easy it is to break the deeply rooted human bond of gratitude.

When we trade thanks with someone, we communicate our belief in her value, her altruism, and the importance of her place in our group. Thanking someone acknowledges her strength and power as a benefactor and that she need not be angry, envious, or suspicious that we see her as anything else. On a fundamental level, each of us wants and needs to be valued by someone else. In fact, our brains have evolved in response to this fundamental survival strategy of being part of a group: being successful at home, work, and play is about being involved with other people in mutually productive relationships. On the neurobiological level, this positive social interaction triggers the release of neuropeptides such as oxytocin, inspiring a mutually positive feeling between the participants of the exchange. We have evolved a brain that desires to be seen as valuable.

As a psychiatrist who works with both adults and adolescents disadvantaged by addiction and mental illness, I have seen every form of anger a human being can manifest, from seething envy to desperate, impotent rage. I have seen the damage and pain that can result when anger goes unmitigated. Anger, long hardwired in our brain for survival, is not going away anytime soon. But what you do with this powerful emotion is completely up to you. You actually have more control over how your anger plays out than you think you do, especially once you learn to recognize, listen to, and then think about your anger. You do have a choice of the path you take in response to your angry feelings. It is in this shift from feeling to thinking where you will find the tools to transform your anger and, as important, the anger of others.

The techniques I'm sharing have emerged after years of observation, coupled with the translation and application of my colleagues' research. I have brought the lab bench to the bedside to create emotion-regulating tools for my patients, tools that have enabled them to recognize and understand their feelings, measure their responses, and help them create positive results. These seven strategies, grounded in the latest neuroscience and psychological data, have the capacity to influence every aspect of a person's life.

Within each of us is the power to transform anger into something quite positive. *Outsmarting Anger* is an emotional survival kit everyone ought to have.

CHAPTER 1

A Glimpse into the Angry Brain

If you are patient in one moment of anger,
you will escape a hundred days of sorrow.

—Chinese proverb

Many years ago, before I went to medical school, I had the chance to visit New York City, a much bigger city than Boston, my hometown. I marveled at the skyscrapers and the density of noise and people. I recall walking down the street feeling the energy and excitement of the place. My eyes wandered for a moment and made contact with another person standing in front of a building. He was taller and more muscular than I, wearing a white tank-top shirt that seemed to purposely display his gym-jacked arms and shoulders.

"What you looking at?" he sneered.

In the blink of an eye, my brain registered that this stranger, at whom I'd simply glanced, was threatening me. His posture looked menacing, his eyes widened, and his muscles appeared to tense and ripple. In the next blink of an eye, part of me began to feel angry. Who was this guy to say anything to me, a complete stranger? But I had other things to do rather than engage this person. I wanted to dismiss any thought in his mind that I posed a threat, because I didn't want or need a fight. And besides, I was half his size. "Nothing," I replied, trying to defuse what was clearly a threatening remark.

"Who you calling nothing?" he menaced. He was looking to escalate, but I wasn't interested. Intuitively I chose to move out of what he perceived as his territorial boundary, picked up my pace, looked away, and said no more. But the fact that this man said anything to me made me angry.

This simple exchange may sound familiar. When a person is faced with a threat of any kind, it is human nature to either confront or run away, approach or avoid—what we commonly call "fight or flight." In mere milliseconds, my brain registered a huge number of factors: New York City was terra incognita, and I was a tourist; this man had large, tattoo-emblazoned biceps; and I had tickets for a Broadway show that night that I didn't want to miss due to a street fight over "nothing." The other man's brain was also assessing quickly that I was not in fact a threat to him, simply a curious spectator, and that it was safe to magnify his angry and menacing response, "Who you calling nothing?" His words kept the distance between us, his body stance a signal to move on, and I took that option, looked away, and kept walking.

Once clear of a threat, we usually put these instances out of our minds. But I began to wonder what exactly it was that made him angry, and then what made me angry. After all, I hadn't yelled at him or brandished a weapon. He hadn't actually moved one of his ferocious-looking muscles. Then I realized that in fact it was quite simple. It was his emotional state—his *anger*. His anger, more than his words, signaled instantly, "Shove off, man. Your glance is not welcome here." What had I done to elicit anger in this stranger? Somehow the way I looked at him, the movement of my body, the words I spoke combined to influence his response.

Often, people will smile when you catch their gaze. But sometimes, for a host of reasons, some people respond from a place of anger-fueled hostility. What got them there rarely has to do directly with you, but emerges as a response to you. You just happened upon them at an inopportune moment, and they reacted coolly or aggressively just because you looked them in the eye, took a parking spot they wanted, or even tried to be friendly. But when we do face these encounters, we also come to witness a great natural force, one that we all have ticking inside us: anger. I believe we have the ability to transform anger, once a primitive force of potential destruction and injury, into a powerful and beneficial resource. When we learn to outsmart our anger, we can unlock the infinite potential we all have inside us. But first, we must get to know this powerhouse of an emotion.

ANGER IS ONLY AN EMOTION

Though we often associate the two, anger is not aggression. Aggression is the enactment of anger and can take many forms, physical and verbal. Anger, however, is an emotion, a feeling. There is an odd irony that anger is in the same club of emotions as joy and love, because it can feel so utterly different, easily igniting aggression with the right conditions. Under its spell, we can feel like a pumped up, steroid-injected alter ego whom we don't recognize later on. On one end of the spectrum, anger can be the source of festering stress. On the other, anger can be the fuel for violence and destruction, even death.

Anger is so strong that it has the capacity to change others' behavior. No other human emotion has the capacity to bend the will of another the way anger can, especially when anger turns to aggression. I certainly hightailed it away from that New York muscleman. Anger expressed in this way is like the growl of a lion in the wild. This kind of anger creates fear, the effect of which is to scare off an intruder or predator. The approach of "fight" can induce an avoidance reaction of flight.

But the emotion of anger that we often experience as humans is not always, or even usually, expressed as outward and violent aggression. Unlike lions, humans do not act on instinct alone. Often, people turn these emotions inward to later surface as depression or bitterness. In my work as a psychiatrist with children and adults, I frequently discover that repressed anger has turned into a sense of powerlessness, stress, frustration, or disapproval. Many of these people are experiencing anger and do not know how to express or handle this very powerful emotion. Anger can rankle in the human brain and manifest in many other, destructive ways that we will explore later in this chapter. Anger's power over us individually is immense, and its ripple effect throughout all aspects of our lives—our relationships, careers, educational experiences, health—can be life altering, even devastating.

Yet just as potent is our innate ability to understand and control the forces of anger in ourselves and others. Think back to the last time you were extremely angry. Did you use strong language, yell, or strike? Although it may seem that these responses are spontaneous and uncontrollable, each one is actually profoundly under your control. You have a choice of what to do and how to express your anger.

This ability to choose develops as we grow older. If you're a parent, you have seen how anger can consume a toddler who can't reach or have something he's after. You have had to step in, change the course of your child's behavior, and redirect his emotions. You are slowly showing your child how anger can be controlled. Anger control is expected of adults, although of course it doesn't always happen. Often the angry person appears to be out of control and his actions unpredictable. Their unpredictability can make us anxious, and activates in us the avoidance of flight or the approach of fight. But there is another choice we can make.

We can wonder, *What is it about that person's inner life that is making him angry?* When you get beyond the shouts and gesticulations, you find that angry people are frequently deeply frustrated over something that seems not so important in retrospect: having someone cut them off in traffic, or a person seeming rude and inconsiderate. Perhaps, ironically, their own fear over the loss of something drove their emotions to detonate, causing them to lose the thing they wanted after all. Uncovering what is really making you or another person angry is key to figuring out how to defuse that anger.

When we understand the evolution of anger, and the reasons this natural force remains a determinant of human behavior, we can learn to expose it and use it. Not only that, but like the martial arts master who uses the energy of the opponent to power his own moves, each of us has the ability to detect, harness, and train the force of anger in ourselves and others. When we do this, we can apply it in ways that enhance our lives, achieve our goals, and, ultimately, influence other people's behavior for the better as well.

ALL BRAINS ARE BUILT BASICALLY THE SAME

We all know on a deep gut level what anger feels like. It can be a gradual or sudden tide of emotion, the sensation of which seems to invade every cell. Our breathing speeds up, we sweat, our faces flush, and our eyes can lose focus. In fact, the whole body can spring into action as our testosterone level, heart rate, and blood pressure surge. All of these body responses are activated by anger, which stems from the most ancient and primitive parts of our brain.

One of my favorite descriptions of the human brain comes from neuroscientist David Linden. In an apt and colorful metaphor, Linden explains that the brain is like a "three-scoop ice cream cone," as illustrated in Figure 1.1. These "scoops" are the brain stem, the limbic system, and the neocortex. This three-tiered structure is the current pinnacle of human brain evolution, and recent brain research has allowed scientists to observe that in fact, the assembly of all human brains is basically the same.

Starting at the base of the brain is the first scoop, the brain stem, which flows down into the spinal cord. This is the most ancient part of the brain, responsible for critical bodily functions like heart rate and breathing, which are automatic. In all creatures, a well-functioning brain stem is crucial to both its immediate and evolutionary survival.

Millions of years ago, the second scoop, the limbic system, evolved. Curved like a ram's horn and resting right on top of the brain stem, this section contains the right and left amygdalae and is the home of

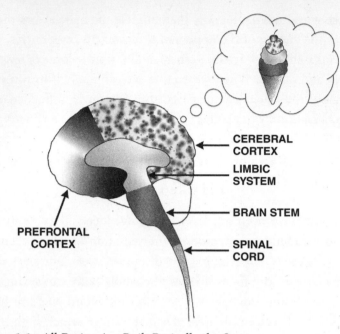

Figure 1.1. All Brains Are Built Basically the Same
Illustration by Sophia T. Shrand.

our impulses, memory, and our seven basic emotions: anger, contempt, fear, disgust, joy, sadness, and surprise. These core emotions are the foundation of the enormous range of our feelings from annoyance and rage to depression, remorse, and guilt. The limbic system is also the source of our fight-or-flight response, and because of this basic survival component, we often refer to the limbic system as the "lizard brain." In fact, I often describe extreme anger as "going limbic." The emotional responses generated in the limbic system are sent to many areas of the brain, in particular to the third scoop—the neocortex, or "new brain."

Made up of one hundred billion cells, the neocortex of humans and all animals with backbones (vertebrates) is the location of higher brain functions, such as vision, language, and sensory abilities. But

THE LONELY IGUANA

When we describe "lizard brain" behaviors, what we're really referring to are raw, instinctual survival behaviors driven by such factors as food, territory, safety, and mating. Stimuli such as fear, mayhem, and revenge—the staple ingredients of Hollywood blockbusters—appeal to our lizard brain.

What makes a real lizard brain different from ours is that it lacks a prefrontal cortex, the part of the brain that makes rational thought possible. Reptiles do of course have a limbic system, allowing them to respond to their environments and preserve their own lives. But unlike humans, they do not experience emotion as we know it. Emotions are in essence an attribution of language, and it is unlikely that a lizard is aware of feeling "angry" or "sad" or "happy" because it does not use human language to describe sensations.

Many reptile owners will swear that their snakes and iguanas show emotion. Dr. Michel Cabanac of Quebec seems to have shown that they are correct. Cabanac, who writes about the evolution of consciousness, published a series of papers reporting that an iguana's heart rate increased from 70 to 110 beats per minute with gentle handling, but the heart rate of frogs did not. He speculated that this mild stress of handling could be an "emotional" response. Fear, indeed, would incite the fight-or-flight response, increasing heart rate. Cabanac's research has also shown that all reptiles, birds, and mammals are driven by the search for pleasure, and this drive for pleasure often overcomes all other desires. Perhaps then an anger response, deriving from the belief that someone else is doing something we do not like (displeasure), is our way of attempting to turn the situation to a more pleasurable one.

our neocortex is called the new brain for another reason: the development of "advanced cognition." Advanced cognition literally means a more complicated way of thinking, a process that involves memory, analyzing current information in the context of those memories, and formulating a plan to address the current situation. In particular, a relatively newly evolved section of the neocortex called the prefrontal cortex, or PFC, has been recognized as the brain's "executive" center and the major brain region involved in this advanced thinking ability. Our PFC, located just behind the forehead, helps us solve problems, make decisions, and anticipate the consequences of those decisions—think things through. Humans' ability to process and tame the deep and primitive emotions and impulses that radiate from the limbic system comes from the PFC, represented by the cherry on top of the ice-cream cone. It is this compact brain section that truly distinguishes us as human beings. Although other animals have some ability to plan, strategize, empathize, and perhaps even think creatively, human beings have developed and applied these attributes to build cities, cultures, international institutions of trade and commerce, countless machines and tools, currency, the Internet—all activities that stem from the PFC.

Although the PFC is the most advanced part of the brain, it is also the last to mature in humans and takes decades to acquire full function. Following the brain's evolutionary trajectory, it is the brain stem and limbic system that develop first. Human infants can squirm around in their bassinets and express emotion, but they can't yet slam-dunk a basketball. The motor cortex, the part of the brain that controls muscles, slowly develops over time. The maturation of the PFC takes longer, which explains in large part why the teenagers we live with seem so emotional, irrational, and impulsive at times. In fact, the PFC is not fully developed in humans until well into the twenties, and may continue to mature and change throughout our lifetime. But given stressful conditions, such as fatigue and hunger, we are all prone to "limbic" moments when we have a harder time thinking straight.

THE PFC: THE KEY TO PERSONALITY

Many parts of the body are divided into sections called lobes, such as the earlobe or the different lobes of the brain. In the back of the brain is the occipital lobe; the middle of the brain is the parietal lobe; toward the side and bottom of the brain is the temporal lobe; and at the front of the brain, the frontal lobe. Each section has its own particular function and evolution, but they are intimately interconnected and have an impact and influence on one another.

More than a century before fMRI studies allowed scientists to see into the brain, a number of medical doctors believed that they had evidence that the front portion of the brain was critical to how a person behaved and controlled his or her response: gently or with anger, boldly or with fear. Some of this evidence originated from the nearly fatal accident of a young railroad worker named Phineas Gage. In the mid-1800s, the transcontinental railroad was being built across the United States, and Phineas Gage was one of the workers who was helping build it. His job was to use an iron tamping rod to pack gunpowder into rocks so that they could be blasted and then removed to make room for track. Phineas was a happy family man who had a kind and gentle way with people. One day in 1848, a spark from the iron rod suddenly ignited the gunpowder. In an instant, the massive three-foot-seven-inch-long bar of iron rocketed into Gage's head, entering his skull just beneath the socket of his left eye and exiting through the right top of his skull (see Figure 1.2). Amazingly, Gage survived, and with time he recovered physically, but the massive brain injury he suffered changed his demeanor forever.

Now, having a huge piece of iron shattering through one's skull would probably change anyone, but there was more to it than the trauma of the event. Reports of his life in the years after his injury suggested that he was never quite the same man. Although his neurological abilities returned, his family and friends reported his behavior and personality to be completely different. A kind man became a

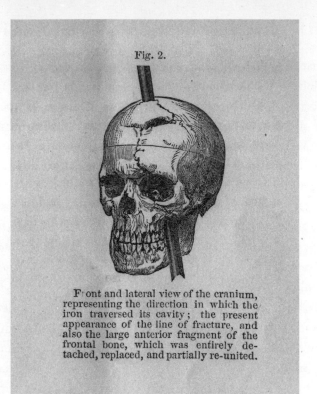

Fig. 2.

F⸱ont and lateral view of the cranium, representing the direction in which the iron traversed its cavity; the present appearance of the line of fracture, and also the large anterior fragment of the frontal bone, which was entirely detached, replaced, and partially re-united.

Figure 1.2. Phineas Gage
Source: From "Recovery from the Passage of an Iron Bar Through the Head," by J. M. Harlow, 1868, *Publications of the Massachusetts Medical Society, 2,* pp. 327–347.

surly man. A gentle man became an angry man with a short fuse and little tolerance. The brain damage that occurred was largely in the PFC, and this apparently left him unable to control his impulses. As Dr. John Martyn Harlow, his attending physician, later wrote, there was no longer a balance between his "intellectual faculties and animal propensities."

In the twentieth century, psychiatrists and neurologists would learn more about the PFC through the development and use of the frontal lobotomy. (In medicine, the suffix -*tomy* at the end of a word implies cutting, such as in an appendectomy, when the appendix is cut out of the body. A lobotomy is literally the cutting of a lobe, in this case the front section of the brain, hence the term "frontal lobotomy.") First popularized by Portuguese physician and neurologist António Egas Moniz, who would go on to win a Nobel Prize in medicine for this work, the lobotomy appeared to offer relief to patients with severe mental illness who displayed erratic behaviors. By reaching into the brain's frontal lobes, the surgeon would then cut tissue connecting the PFC to the thalamus. The result of this procedure flattened or "tamed" the emotional outbursts and was thought to be a benefit to patients and caregivers. Worldwide, surgeons performed tens of thousands of lobotomies, until the advent of more effective and less invasive antipsychotic medications in the 1950s. Controversial as they became, lobotomies also verified to the medical community the location of the personality, higher cognitive ability, and impulse control, as well as the ability to initiate—the PFC.

But although events in history instructed us usefully as to where specific brain abilities were located, the dark side of the lobotomy's impact is that people who had their frontal lobes dissected were not just docile: they were often robbed of the human creative process, and possibly the ability to experience all emotions consciously. Some were left incapacitated for life, including such notables as Rosemary, the sister of John F. Kennedy, and Rose, the older sister of Tennessee Williams. In the clarity of retrospect, we now see the insult done to the humanity of an individual when the prefrontal lobes are damaged through accident or cut with "therapeutic" surgery.

Of course, today's exciting neuroimaging technology helps us see this area as it works, unraveling more of its secrets each day. But there is still great room for exploration and development on how to tap in to the power of the PFC to affect behavior, especially our powerful anger response and impulse. The way we can control anger is simple, effective, and basically free; it is already within us all, just waiting to be applied. These steps are described in the following chapters. But first, let's look at anger itself as a part of our evolutionary heritage.

ANGER AS PROTECTOR

Let's add this component to our definition of anger: anger is an emotion designed to change someone else's behavior and sometimes even one's own. For example, we get angry at ourselves when we bang our finger with a hammer or if we feel we have put on too much weight. But while anger can be a great motivator to change our own behavior, it has been used over and over again to change the behavior of someone else. My interaction with the man in New York was a great example.

The stranger I glanced at did not want me to look, and sent a clear message of anger to get me to change. And I responded. That so much information could be received and processed and then generate a response in that split second is due to our remarkable brain. When my eyes unintentionally met the angry gaze of that stranger in New York, information came streaming through my optic nerve, activating parts of my limbic system, which attributed a feeling and intention to the person. A message was sent to my PFC, alerting me that I needed to make a plan. The stranger could be dangerous. How did I know this? Because plain as day, it was right there on his face.

The face is among the most important clues to what another person is thinking or feeling. As such, the human face takes on enormous importance in orienting us to people we encounter. On a deep brain level, an angry face is one that we have evolved to avoid, according to a team of scientists from the Netherlands. The researchers compared the gazes of adults with those of four- and seven-month-old infants. All were shown pictures of angry faces, and their eye movements were recorded and analyzed. The findings, published in the journal *Cognition & Emotion*, revealed that all the age groups avoided dwelling on angry faces, but surprisingly, the adults in particular avoided looking at the eyes of an angry face. We avoid eye contact with angry faces as we get older because we have learned that doing so might be dangerous. When I inadvertently looked into the eyes of the stranger, I was breaking a deep evolutionary rule.

In that moment, I needed to make a decision about what to do. What were his intentions? Was I strong enough to win if he tried to attack me? Was I fast enough to run away if I didn't think I would win? And his brain did the same, attributing intention to me. My direct, albeit fleeting, gaze into his angry face was a confrontation of sorts. This dance between fear and anger, the two faces of threat, has occurred billions of times since the dawn of our human wakening. Ancient, instantaneous, and elegant in their effectiveness, these critical emotions have helped us survive.

As a consequence, both fear and anger have thrived and evolved as strong, dynamic, even fascinating emotions. When we are afraid, we hope the danger passes, or we want to run away. But when we are angry, something very different happens: we want or need to change the behavior of someone else. To do this, the brain has to work hard and work differently. That was the hypothesis of French researchers who analyzed the fMRI studies of subjects who were provoked into both fear and anger. Their results, published in the journal *Neuro-Image*, showed that in fact, the angry brain goes into a more complex organizational mode than the fearful brain.

Common sense suggests why this might be so: if you are angry, one step away from aggression, you have to process more information. Just as you would when planning a chess game at high speed, you have to anticipate what your opponent is going to do, and mobilize your rapid response. The amygdalae—the parts of the brain involved in emotional memory—are activated, in order to draw on past experience. If you are about to be attacked, you have to prepare your body to respond. Your motor cortex is responsible for getting your arms and legs (and all your muscles) to move in a coordinated way (see Figure 1.3). And there is a part of your brain recruited into action even before the actual physical response is performed: the premotor cortex helps initiate your next move. But if the premotor cortex is preparing you for how to respond, it is also a response itself to your anticipating the next move of your opponent. Responsibility for that anticipation is located in your PFC.

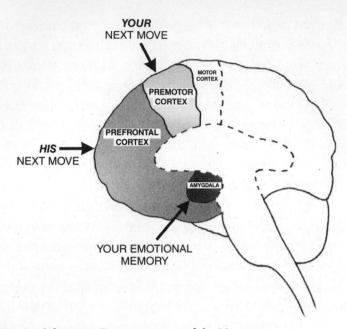

Figure 1.3. Schematic Representation of the Neocortex
Illustration by Sophia T. Shrand.

Anger can be perceived as a highly evolved emotion, drawing
instantly on multiple areas of the brain. A sophisticated anger response
meant survival for primitive humans. Anger was protective; its threat
could keep competitors and predators at bay. Sounds like something
that we wouldn't want to altogether eliminate. But now, in the twenty-
first century, our prehistoric urges do not always serve us in the way
we would like, and can even be an impediment. Research has shown
that when we are angry, we are more likely to miss information than
when we are afraid. This would make sense, as our angry brain is too
busy assessing our opponent's actions. But in today's world, throwing
a tantrum when operating a motor vehicle doesn't ensure survival.
Screaming at a customer service rep is not scaring away a hungry
predator. And smashing your keyboard is not going to provide evidence of great strength. These behaviors are not effective survival

responses of modern humanity, and are instead often counterproductive. So why do we still get angry?

THE THREE DOMAINS

Although it seems as though humans get upset and angry over many different types of things, a close analysis reveals that in fact there are primarily three core reasons that we become angry. We experience a threat to one of what I call the *three domains:* our resources, our residence, and our relationships—or, in loose translation, food, shelter, and mate. Within each of these categories is a subset of specific needs key for survival that we attempt to meet and for which we must compete. When we face obstacles or threats having to do with access to these needs, we become angry. As already noted, anger is an emotion designed to change the behavior of someone else. We want someone to change his or her behaviors so that we can access these basic foundations of our safety, success, and well-being:

1. *Resources:* access to food, money, material goods
2. *Residence:* shelter, home, community, workplace, safety, comfort
3. *Relationships:* close family, mates or potential mates, friendships, employees, employers

Resources

Of the three domains, resources, or what we could call "means," may be the most critical for individual survival: with access to some resources, one can survive; with plentiful resources, one can more easily ensure success in the other two domains. Imagine a typical initial response when someone has become a victim of a Ponzi scheme: it is not going to be sadness. It is going to be anger. His or her resources have been stolen, which in turn affects the other domains, including safety and family security. What was the response to Bernie Madoff when he made off with millions from those trusting people?

A lot—and I mean a lot—of anger. The first reaction included individuals' lashing out against Madoff and demanding to be reimbursed. Ultimately, the community punished him by taking away his possessions and putting him in jail. Madoff cheated and was held accountable by the group. Putting him in jail, in this case, defused at least a little of the anger experienced by those he had swindled.

We've all had similar reactions when someone was taking resources that we thought we had a right to. What would your reaction be when at a restaurant the server ignores your table, serving a few other tables before yours? What happens when two people eye the same parking space and neither wants to give it up?

It is actually remarkable that we share resources at all with anyone who is not part of our direct family. But human beings have learned how to do just this, cooperating to make clothes, build houses, grow and distribute food, and set up shops and markets where one person can buy the goods made by someone else. As the economist Paul Seabright so eloquently points out, we live in a world of strangers, intimately dependent on people we do not even know. He starts his book *The Company of Strangers: A Natural History of Economic Life*, describing all the strangers who contributed to his being able to buy a cotton shirt in a clothing store. One stranger years ago had to plant the cotton. Another stranger harvested the cotton with a machine built by other strangers, who used parts milled by yet other strangers. Eventually more strangers transported the cotton; others wove it into fabric on machines built by strangers; and the shirt, transported by strangers, was placed on a rack where Seabright used a credit card, a promise of a payment in the future, to buy the shirt from yet more strangers.

This is working together as a group. One can only imagine how many people involved in this process experienced anger toward one another for a myriad of reasons. But defusing that anger—by cooperating as a group brought together with the intent of making and selling a shirt—facilitated a coordinated effort that got the job done.

Each individual became more successful, but none of this could have been accomplished if anger had not been outsmarted.

E. O. Wilson, the father of the science of sociobiology, wrote in his recent book that it is the advent of these types of group cooperative relationships that truly drove our human species to our current pinnacle of dominance over the world. We give resources freely to those in our group who are in need. But woe to that person who tries to cheat another out of his or her resources. Anger can ignite in an instant, and retribution can be brutal. We shall return to this idea of group mentality later in the book, and how it can be both a force for progress and a dark danger that flames and fuels anger. As Wilson says, "We have created a Star Wars civilization, with Stone Age emotions, medieval institutions, and god-like technology."

Having resources also makes one more attractive to other people. There is a popular perception that people who have more resources, such as money, appear to be more successful, and a successful person is someone whom others want to be near. And although we generally believe that money won't buy you happiness, having money may actually decrease a person's pain. In a study from Sun Yat-sen University in China, published in *Psychological Science*, subjects who handled plain paper felt more social distress from being excluded from an activity, and felt more physical pain when they put their hand in hot water than if they had held real money instead. In addition, when subjects were just reminded that they had spent money, they felt more social distress and physical pain. In today's world, money is our prime resource, as it symbolizes the ability to gain access to many other resources.

Residence

Our residence is our home, but also, more important, our safety and our family's security. In the United States, many people keep guns to protect their homes; a few thousand years ago, it would have been a spear. A threat even to our personal space—when someone stands too close—makes us nervous. Residence means more than our personal house, condo, apartment, or cardboard box under a bridge: residence is our larger community, our town and city, even our nation. Americans experienced an enormous rage on 9/11 when the Twin Towers in New York City were attacked. Our residence had been violated, and the result was a war, whether justified or not. We wanted the perceived attackers to stop trying to hurt our residence.

Each of us lives in some community, be it a big city or a small town, in an urban or suburban setting. How we protect our home environment may depend on our neighbors. There is a reason for the saying "Good fences make for good neighbors." We want our neighbors close, but also separated enough for us to maintain our own homes. We need our personal space; when this is encroached upon we get defensive, and anger is a form of defense.

Being part of the group makes you feel good and makes you feel better about yourself in general. From the point of view of our ancestors, this makes sense; being part of a group is protective, keeping potential danger away or at least enabling one to defend against danger if it appears. During our early evolution, the greatest threats were not necessarily from other species of animal but rather from marauding bands of humans seeking our resources. Membership in a group, a community, a residence, was very comforting. So residence is a major component of what we want to have and preserve as human beings. It is safer to be part of an in-group, and our in-group will help protect us from the advances of an out-group that may be trying to steal our resources.

Communities can bind people together for a common good, but often this affiliation is based on the identification of a potential but shared enemy. Researchers from the University of Marburg in Germany explored this "group mentality." They found that being part of a group enables the outward expression of anger. According to the German study, participants in "collective action" were more likely to perform potentially "radical" behaviors. This finding is supported in many other studies, where group mentality can become mob mentality. We have all experienced or witnessed this phenomenon, even in small ways. Perhaps you were the kid picked on in school, and other kids joined in to tease you. Maybe you have been involved in local community politics and tried to rally a group of like-minded citizens to pass a funding project against the wishes of other citizens who did not want to spend the money. This group mentality, an aspect of our residence, can be productively harnessed to promote peace and yield fruitful results or unproductively harnessed to promote anger and aggression and yield dangerous and destructive outcomes.

The impact of these first two domains, our resources and our residence, often influence the third domain, the one where anger itself may be detonated or defused: the domain of relationships.

Relationships

Have you ever been jealous that your friend has a partner but you don't? How about thinking that your boss likes your coworker more than you? Or that someone else is being treated as a "teacher's pet"? The relationships in our lives are critical to our personal sense of well-being, and when they are threatened, we can become very, very angry. The newspapers are full of stories of jealous rages that lead to murder. We even romanticize them as "crimes of passion." If, as I believe, at the core of every person is the need simply to be valued by another person, then this domain of relationships takes on as much significance as the material domain of resources and the community domain of residence.

In fact, our relationships are intimately connected to our PFC. From this region stems our fundamental human ability to appreciate what another person is thinking or feeling. Called *theory of mind* (ToM), this basic sensitivity develops very early, perhaps as young as eighteen months of age, but then progresses in complexity and maturity in the same way that a squirming baby grows up to be a slam-dunking teen. Our relationships are completely dependent on ToM.

When this ability to understand the motivations of other people is not developing in a child, child psychiatrists worry that he or she may have some form of autism or Asperger's syndrome.

Relationships can make us feel either victoriously valuable or despairingly devalued. They are a source of protection from the outside world of danger, but, more important, they are a source of reaffirmation of our own value and self-worth. We covet the relationships of others and can become protective and territorial in regard to the relationships we have.

All three of these domains, the 3R's of resources, residence, and relationships, influence all of us all the time. And because they are at the core of our survival, we become frustrated and angry when our access to them is blocked. We want those blocks to be gone, and our anger is the emotion most likely to effect this change, whether the obstacles are real, perceived, or even imagined. As you proceed through this book, you will begin to notice the small, almost insignificant angers triggered on a daily basis by one of the three domains.

"PREFRONTAL COP"

We cannot change our brain, but we can learn to use our brain to change our behavior, and we do this with our PFC. Although PFC technically stands for the prefrontal cortex, let's be creative and use the letters to stand for "prefrontal cop." As you've discovered, we have in our brain a tool to police those deeper limbic-driven feelings that can distort reality around us. We have to use our prefrontal cop like a detective to tease out the clues that lead us to feel angry, assess what it is we want someone to do differently or to begin doing that he or she is not, and then as a policeman to enforce law and order—to not submit to the primitive temptation to lash out in anger and try to harm or get rid of whatever is getting us mad (which is sometimes a person we love or at the very least are trying to impress).

The use of the prefrontal cop is also important because it pushes us to assess the situation, process information, generate a plan, execute that plan, and then anticipate the consequences of our actions. When you use your PFC, you're also practicing ToM: empathy and the ability to appreciate what someone else is thinking and feeling. Personally, I do not think it is a coincidence that these two functions of the PFC so critical to our survival, our ability to anticipate the consequence of our actions and ToM, are housed so close together. Somewhere in the course of human psychological development, it probably became really important for me to know how my actions were going to impact you. Would my actions stimulate your limbic system to get your back up in anger and aggression? Would my actions get you to back off and change? Or would my actions convince you that we have each other's backs, that we're in this together, and that we can cooperate instead of compete?

Your PFC is the key to transforming anger—to moving from conflict into cooperation. When you train yourself to tap in to the power of your brain's PFC, you can recognize, police, and modulate your anger response. By practicing this technique, you learn how to rein in stress and anxiety, you are slower to anger, and you avail yourself of more time to contemplate the results of acting on your anger. This way, you turn your anger into something more powerful and productive.

EXERCISING YOUR PFC: THE CASE OF ROAD RAGE

Road rage, a phenomenon that has been studied extensively by researchers over the last decade, is a terrific window into anger. Road rage is a relatively common experience; about one out of three drivers have experienced it at some time. But my suspicion is that the rate is much higher than that; some people may not want to admit to it or may not even recognize that they get angry at all. (I will come back to this in Chapter Two, Recognize Rage.)

Scientists in Spain interviewed twenty-five hundred people and found that road rage decreased with age (perhaps because of PFC maturity), increased with the amount of driving (because of either fatigue or the higher potential for events), and was highest in men and in towns with over ten thousand people. One could speculate that in smaller towns, the chances are higher that you would encounter the other driver at some time in another setting. It is probably not a good idea to be actively threatening someone with whom you are likely to come in contact later. But perhaps when there are more than ten thousand people, that chance of encounter decreases, unfortunately removing a natural barrier and inhibition to one's road rage. The study did offer some encouraging data; only 2.6 percent of the events were perpetrated by "serious" aggressors.

The same incidence, one-third of drivers experiencing road rage, was also reported by researchers at Wright State University in Ohio. Again, only 2 percent or fewer incidents resulted in serious damage to people or cars. Whether in Spain or Ohio, the people most likely to get heated while driving were young men. What's most troubling about road rage is the vengeance component. In Australia, researchers found that of 1,208 drivers who reported road rage, two-thirds of them had been victims of road rage themselves. Anger can beget anger, an important fact to remember as you begin to learn how to recognize and harvest this most basic of emotions.

This road rage story may seem familiar. But as you read about Hank, plug it in to what you now know about the 3R's: resources, residence, and relationships. What was the resource, residence, or relationship that Hank felt was being jeopardized, leading him to his rage? What did he want someone to do differently? What about his decisions? And what part of the brain did Hank use, or not use?

One Monday morning, Hank was late for work, and he got caught in a traffic jam. When he was cut off at the intersection, he honked and screamed at the driver. As another driver tried to cut in front of him, he slammed on the brakes, grabbed a bat out of the backseat, jumped out of the car, and bashed in the other car's windshield. The police were called, and Hank was arrested and taken away in handcuffs.

As the story illustrates, Hank did not have a choice about *feeling* angry. We all experience anger in situations like this. But Hank did have a choice about how his anger played out. If Hank had used his PFC, he would probably have just kept driving. He would have *recognized* that he wanted the other person not to cut him off, and with this awareness would probably have been able to dismiss it as unworthy of mind-numbing rage.

Here's how Hank's reaction can be plugged in to the three domains: he believed that the highway was a limited resource, that the other driver was preventing him from getting to work (residence), that the other driver was potentially humiliating him in front of others (relationships), or some combination of these. Next time you experience road rage, try to move control of your brain from this primitive limbic survival response to the PFC, the new bastion for our more mature survival.

The anonymity of driving is deceptive, just like the anonymity of the Internet, text messaging, even voice mail. This anonymity is not benign, and it contributes to the unleashing of these primitive rages. What is missing in each of these scenarios? Faces. What happens during road rage? In part, we have no brake (pun intended) on our anger. What if Hank had seen the face of the driver, not just the tail end of the car cutting him off? The eye-to-eye contact I had with the Manhattan muscleman presented me with choices, and I chose to see the Broadway show rather than get in a fight. The muscleman made a choice as well, and chose not to pursue me for a fight. In those brief but powerful moments of face-to-face assessment, an act of physical aggression was considered and redirected. My actions to divert removed a critical stimulus to his potential for aggression. But Hank, encased in his machinery, was lacking the eye contact and lacking the actual relational component of direct human interaction, and his anger went unchecked.

Perhaps Hank had been cut off one too many times, and this was the last straw. Perhaps he was late for work and did not want to be embarrassed or get in trouble with his boss. Perhaps he had just gotten a phone call for an overdue credit card payment. Perhaps other stressors left him raw and vulnerable, ready to lash out. But his anger, no matter what the reason, remains his responsibility, and he will be held accountable for his actions.

In what ways could you start exercising your PFC today? Begin to notice how long it takes you to get angry in general. Notice other people when they are getting frustrated or mad. Ask yourself why they became frustrated. Considering that anger is an emotion designed to change the behavior of someone else, what did they need to see someone else do or not do to induce an anger response? Which of their three domains was threatened? Keep these questions in mind. By simply noticing, you are beginning to exercise your PFC. In the next chapter, we will begin to take these observations and learn how to *recognize rage*.

CHAPTER 2

Recognize Rage

When anger rises, think of the consequences.

—Confucius (551–479 BC)

The ultimate value of life depends upon awareness and the power of contemplation rather than upon mere survival.

—Aristotle (384 BC–322 BC)

Eight-year old Billy was playing a board game with nine-year old Jenny, and he could see that she was cheating. But she wouldn't admit it. At stake was a cool prize, a book about orangutans, Billy's favorite animal. As the game proceeded, his face began to redden, and sweat appeared on his brow. His muscles seemed to tense and expand under his T-shirt. The excitement on his face had long since faded. Now his nose was wrinkled, his eyebrows were furrowed, and his lips formed a perfect snarl. When Jenny cheated again and won the game, he clenched his game piece and shook his head. With the raised arms of a triumphant champion, Jenny gave a war whoop and turned to the man in the grey sweater, who handed her the book. Billy knew the outcome of this game was not fair, but what he didn't know was that it had actually been rigged.

Child psychologists were carefully observing his every reaction. Billy, along with 257 other second-graders, was part of a study looking at the ways children control their anger. What the researchers found has exciting and broad implications for how not only children but also adults can learn to identify and then maintain full control over their anger response.

To recognize rage sounds simple. Of course you can tell when someone is angry. It's obvious, right? You've seen people scream at the customer service desk or felt the ire of fans when the ump makes a bad call or had someone yell at you with or without reason. Although universally viewed as socially unacceptable, aggression and "bad tempers" run rampant in our daily lives. Small angers can lead to snippy remarks. Large angers can lead to murder or war. Each of us probably experiences at least a little anger every day. Remarkably, however, most of us do not maim or kill each other regularly. We have, over time, found a way to control those primitive, murderous rages we inherited from our ancestors.

But do we really recognize the full spectrum of the anger response, or just the outburst, the tip of the iceberg? Why don't we ever seem to notice *before* someone suddenly "snaps"? And how many of us can really recognize details of our own anger response? Have you ever impulsively said something mean and harsh, perhaps biting and condescending? Have you ever slammed a door, broken a dish, or kicked a vending machine? Have you ever hit something or someone? Those are aggressive acts fueled by anger. But when did your anger start, and how did you fail to control it?

Although we are indeed born to experience the emotion of anger, the fact is, recognizing and understanding anger and what do with it comes much later. The reason for this is twofold. First, anger is an emotion with a wide spectrum ranging from mild annoyance to aggravation, all the way up to boiling rage. Second, although we are born with the ability to experience and act out our anger, we are *not* born with the ability to monitor our anger response or to "take it down a notch." The ability to modify our emotions, particularly anger, is actually pretty sophisticated and comes with the brain's biological growth and especially the development of the PFC. With maturation of our PFC, this cortical part of our brain can modify and regulate emotions generated from the subcortical limbic part of our brain.

STRESS AND ANGER—WHAT'S THE DIFFERENCE?

Stress is a psychological and physical reaction caused by daily triggers large and small, internal (worry) and external (the bad driver who cuts you off). Your body responds physically when there is a demand on you, and depending on the type of trigger, you experience varying degrees of the fight-or-flight sensation. The body releases vital hormones to prepare you for action, among them adrenaline and cortisol. These chemicals prime your body physically when there is a true, corporeal threat and you must fight or run. At its root, the stress response is a vital, survival-oriented physical response shared by humans and animals.

So is anger. You feel and express anger because there is a threat to one or more of the three domains and you need to change the behavior of the perpetrator or remove the obstacle. So anger is not just a negative emotion, but can be a general response to the threatening triggers of a clear target. When you feel angry, you usually know the cause: the boss who criticized you in a meeting, the partner who let you down, or the neighbor's kid who gave your kid a bloody nose. Anger in those instances is the intense and aggressive feeling of wanting or needing to change the dynamic of the threat, which often means another person's behavior.

Feeling stressed in general is fertile ground for anger, as the body is already revving for action. The person who is successfully managing stress in his life is more likely to be able to control his feelings of anger. The stressed-out person is the one you want to avoid if she experiences anger. Too often the object of this person's wrath will not be the actual "threat."

(continued)

> Instead, the anger is displaced onto the source of a much more minor stress trigger. Unfortunately, we all have done this—snapped crossly at a child, a partner, or a parent who just happened to be in our way when we got home from a dreadful day. Stress fuels it, but anger makes it happen.

Imagine a child's tantrum over a trinket. As adults, we may wonder why a child becomes so angry over what seems so insignificant. But that trinket is not insignificant to the toddler. From his or her point of view, it seems a critical and vital resource. The child's PFC is relatively immature, and his or her limbic emotional brain is more dominant. But in an anger situation, no matter how old your brain may be, that limbic, emotional, impulsive portion always has the potential to take over and launch your rage. You gain control of your anger when you shift back to the PFC, and that is why the first step in managing your anger is to recognize that you are angry at all. Recognition is a function of the PFC.

When you recognize rage, you learn to use your PFC to identify the feeling of anger *within yourself* well before you act. Whether you're irritated at a late train, vexed over a slow Internet connection, or infuriated with a colleague, the ability to pinpoint your limbic anger is a decisive determinant of success. Although controlling the limbic system is not necessarily innate, the brain tools are all there just waiting to be trained and developed. When you tap in to this strength, you can learn to identify this powerful emotion in others as well, often before they act. Whether you're observing yourself or someone else, it's important to remember that the loose cannons in life don't usually get what they want in the long run. The sooner you learn how to recognize rage, the sooner you'll be able slow down that emotional freight train and prevent a regrettable, even tragic act—yours or that of another person.

DESIGNED FOR ANGER

When a newborn baby arrives in the world, she is born with all the brain stem and limbic machinery to feel angry within a few hours of birth. A hungry infant gets angry that the environment is not satisfying her need for food or comfort. She wails. She wants to be fed. She wants an unknown "something" to do something different. How she signals these needs is an active area of research and appears to be the same across cultures. Mothers notice a baby's cry and attribute meaning to those imploring sounds. Much attention has been paid to the varieties of infant cries—one that may signal hunger, another for discomfort. But an angry cry appears to be uniquely different and distinguishable. In a recent study, Italian researchers found that most women could identify an angry cry in infants who were only four to seven hours old. The "dysphonic," or especially harsh, cry was described as the "angriest."

A research team from Minneapolis was able to show the sequence of anger reactions in fifteen-month-old babies when mothers gently held back their child's arms from a desired toy. The first time, many of these infants struggled against their moms, and those that struggled also cried and protested. But the second time the child was kept back from the toy, the behavior escalated: the struggle began much more quickly and predictably, as if the child had been "primed" for an angry reaction, for an attack. Indeed, that is exactly what is happening. To a toddler, the toy is a resource, and the obstacle is the mother's arms. In essence the toddler is communicating, "Stop holding me back, Mom," as he tries to change his mother's behavior.

When the feeling of anger overtakes you, your body prepares for battle, readying for the "fight" option of "fight or flight." Your muscles tighten, your blood pressure rises, and you breathe more heavily. Blood flows to your limbs and extremities, in preparation for action. In anger, more blood goes to the hands. In fear, more goes to the feet. Meanwhile, the brain is releasing neurotransmitters like noradrenaline, a catecholamine that gives you a sudden burst of energy. As your attention fixates on the threat to your domains, other chemicals like glucocorticoids are flooding your system, getting your body ready to release stored sugars and bringing you to a state of energized readiness. The tension of your muscles gives you the feeling of power and self-confidence. You are now set for battle.

Exercise: Draw This Shape

This is the letter V.

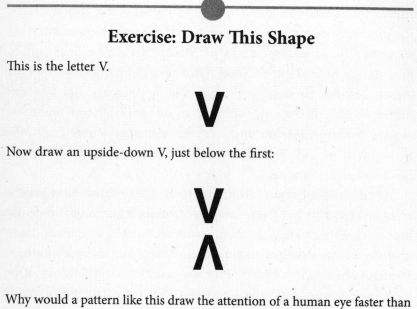

Now draw an upside-down V, just below the first:

Why would a pattern like this draw the attention of a human eye faster than any other? Take a few seconds to wonder about it, then draw an oval around the two V's like this:

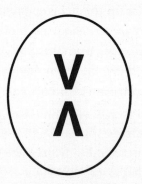

Amazing, isn't it. Our brains are designed to tune in quickly to just the shape and suggestion of an angry face. Now add in a dot on either side of the top V.

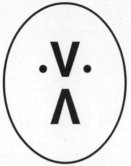

That is an angry face!

Try making an angry face. If you're in a good mood, this may be hard to do, but try it anyway by thinking of something that made you really mad in the past or that would make you mad today. You'll make this same face whether you live in New York or in Tokyo or in Bangladesh, whether in a city, on a farm, in a desert, on an island, or on frozen tundra. Your nose may wrinkle up, your eyebrows will form a V, and your mouth may open wide and bare your teeth in a threat gesture. Your face may actually turn a little red, just like Billy's face when Jenny was so blatantly cheating in the research study. You've made the face, you've seen the face, and you may have even gotten someone else to make the face. The pattern is well known.

This pattern, like the patterns of all emotions, is observable even in the faces of people born without sight. It has become known by social scientists as "the face of anger." This V pattern has also been called the "shape of threat." In 2007, researchers from Michigan State discovered that a downward geometric V pattern alone was all it took for the human brain to detect a threatening, angry face. When the study participants were asked to do a random visual scanning task, they detected this shape fastest from among a field of other shapes. The researchers' conclusion: angry faces can be detected by shape alone. This study was replicated and confirmed in 2011 by a group from the University of Warwick in the United Kingdom. There is no escaping this biological imprint of anger. It has been embedded in human behavior for eons, exquisitely designed to keep aggressors at bay.

RECOGNIZING RAGE IN OURSELVES

As adults, we are expected to have control over our emotions. But not everyone is equal in the ability to process anger. Various genetic and environmental factors influence our tendencies toward anger and how we respond. This was just the question that the University of Delaware scientists were investigating when they rigged the game that Billy and Jenny were playing.

In the three-month study, they made their best effort to incite angry emotions in 257 eight-year-olds by having one child cheat while adult onlookers saw but did nothing about it. They were able to sort the kids' responses by how much their faces expressed anger and how conductive their skin was (a measure of noradrenaline response), as well as by whether the kids could report the feeling of anger.

What they found was that these kids, as early as second grade, could naturally be separated in terms of five basic types of anger experience (summarized in Figure 2.1):

1. Physiology-and-expression controllers (high self-report, low expression, low physiological arousal)
2. Expression-only controllers (high self-report, low expression, high physiological arousal)
3. Noncontrollers (high self-report, high expression, medium physiological arousal)
4. Nonreactive (low self-report, low expression, low physiological arousal)

	PHYSIOLOGY-and-EXPRESSION CONTROLLERS	EXPRESSION-ONLY CONTROLLERS	NONCONTROLLERS	NONREACTIVE	NONREPORTERS
SELF-REPORT	HIGH	HIGH	HIGH	LOW	LOW
EXPRESSION	LOW	LOW	HIGH	LOW	MEDIUM
PHYSIOLOGICAL AROUSAL	LOW	HIGH	MEDIUM	LOW	MEDIUM

Figure 2.1. Profiles of Anger Control in Second-Grade Children
Source: Data from "Profiles of Anger Control in Second-Grade Children: Examination of Self-Report, Observational, and Physiological Components," by M. Smith, J. A. Hubbard, and J. P. Laurenceau, 2011, *Journal of Experimental Child Psychology, 110*, pp. 213–226.
Illustration by Sophia T. Shrand.

5. Nonreporters (low self-report, medium expression, medium physiological arousal)

What most of us mental health professionals have learned through years of seeing how different people handle emotions is that some anger types are actually healthier than others. Anger has never killed anyone: it's what a person does with the anger, or any emotion, that can lead to trouble. Our brains and bodies respond to these emotions, often changing things like our heart rate and blood pressure, which can harm our bodies through heart attacks and strokes. Sometimes we become aggressive, enacting our anger. Our aggression can harm other people's bodies or can have an impact on resources, residence, or relationships. In this way, anger can transform into an exploding bomb, with destructive shrapnel careening out in all directions. But the anger itself, the emotion itself, has never killed anyone.

The types of anger outlined by the study of second-graders creates a scale of response, starting with the healthiest and progressing to the least healthy. Someone in category 1, a physiology-and-expression controller (high self-report, low expression, low physiological arousal), may be quite aware of her emotional experiences but capable of controlling the limbic signals. Whether this person is a child or adult, she is going to be less likely to be provoked into fights or by other button-pushing stimuli that could harm her or get her into trouble. She is using her PFC to outsmart her anger.

Someone in category 2, an expression-only controller (high self-report, low expression, high physiological arousal), will be someone who experiences high levels of emotion, but has the ability to cover it up and not let it show to others; this might be where Billy falls on the continuum. When given the chance to express his experience, this type of person can easily put into words how angry he feels. What he is less in control of or less aware of, however, is the toll his restrained anger has taken on his body. With enormous effort, Billy kept his anger inside, but his heart rate, blood pressure, and skin response were going wild.

Category 3, noncontrollers (high self-report, high expression, medium physiological arousal), are what you might imagine most children to be. They feel their emotions and don't hold back their expression. If they are second-graders, they are still learning to control their urges. If they're adults, we may actually call them "childish." Being hotheaded is OK if you are a kid, but more is expected of the adult PFC to keep those limbic processes in check. The low physiological toll is worth noting, however. This finding suggests that the outward expression of anger, in some cases, may save the inside of your body some wear and tear. What happens to the outside of your body may be another story if you keep getting into physical fights. But being in the first category is still better, and safer too.

Category 4, nonreactive (low self-report, low expression, low physiological arousal) is extremely interesting. One way to understand this finding is that these are folks oblivious to the world around them. They do not seem to notice events that make other people angry. But a more sinister interpretation is that these are the kids, and then adults, who feel so defeated that they do not even try. Why bother responding to a world where you feel powerless? We know about fight and flight. But a third response, when you perceive you are neither fast enough to get away nor strong enough to fight, is to freeze, to do nothing, to become invisible and hope the danger passes. Perhaps this is what the examiners uncovered: those kids who have already given up, tuned out, and shut down. These are kids I absolutely want to see in my office, the sooner the better.

Category 5, the nonreporters (low self-report, medium expression, medium physiological arousal), are children or adults about whom I also worry. This last category is the type of person who may repress her anger so much that she is not even aware that what she felt was anger at all. She might experience an event as stressful and frustrating, but she has not learned to identify the emotion as anger, despite how her body was responding. These are the folks more likely to displace their anger onto the world around them, without a clue as to why they are angry, because they don't see it in themselves.

We all have a friend or two like this, a person who is cranky and edgy but unaware of the motivation behind his somewhat abrasive response. When asked, this person would look incredulous if you suggested he was ticked off. I have a lot of patients like this, for whom anger is not a part of how they see themselves, nor how they want to see themselves. Instead, the people around them walk on eggshells, and the patients themselves are astonished at how lonely they are becoming without much insight into how their own behavior is causing their isolation.

Some anger experts believe that certain individuals are just born with more anger, which manifests as a heightened adrenaline response to stress triggers. These individuals have what has been called "trait" anger; that is, they have a greater tendency to react with anger to certain situations—and to stay angry. Most of us, however, have "state" anger: we respond to triggers, but the anger is a temporary emotional state. Whether you are someone with trait anger or not, it is ultimately the way in which you get your anger out that can keep you safe and out of trouble.

How do you experience this most basic of human emotions? Do you recognize your own anger but keep your cool? Or does your face get flushed and your muscles tense up? Do you feel and recognize anger, but don't express it? Perhaps you are a person who knows you are angry and let's everyone else know it too, getting upset and turning up the heat around you. Maybe you don't react at all, even if you feel a little angry. Or perhaps you are not even aware that you are angry, but your body knows and reacts, manifesting as having a shorter fuse, being more aggressive and generally quick to respond to any perception of insult.

Experiencing intense anger and holding it in can also be dangerous for your health. Researchers in Japan, a nation known for strong emotional control among its people, looked at stress and anger in a group of 6,929 men and women. Those who scored higher on the "anger-in," or suppressed anger, category had a greater chance of increased blood pressure, known to be a leading cause of heart disease and stroke. This study, along with a lot of common sense, suggests that channeling your anger in a healthy way may be better than trying to ignore or suppress it.

As the researchers discovered with the second-graders, some people, even at a tender age, are able to mobilize the PFC to channel the limbic emotion and modify their anger better than others. The PFC is able to anticipate the consequence of acting out in anger and modulate a response. Whatever your circumstances, or variation of trait anger you inherited, learning to identify how you experience anger can be a useful first step in recognizing your own rage. With this self-understanding, you can consciously tap in to the PFC and practice managing anger scenarios. There is a way to just not get as angry. And more, there is a way to help other people not get as

IS IT SNICKERS TIME?

Scientists from Kentucky have shown that people who had more difficulty with glucose control were also more aggressive and prone to violence. These people simply had less behavioral self-control. Self-control, a brain phenomenon, takes a lot of energy to maintain—energy in the form of glucose. So it makes sense that if you have low blood sugar, or less available energy, you may have more difficultly using the PFC to modulate those angry impulses.

It is likely that our ancestors foraged through most of the waking day, nibbling on nuts and berries when they could find them. It would make evolutionary sense that our bodies have adjusted to this way of eating. In our modern world, where we are lucky to find time for any reasonable meal, our blood sugar level is much more erratic. I'm not saying that you should carry around a candy bar, but you should take care of your body and keep your blood sugar stable. Nutritionists often suggest that having a few snacks, such as nuts or fruit, during the day can help. The well-fed brain makes a calmer person.

angry. That's what we will explore starting in Chapter Five, Promote Peace.

WHY DO YOU NEED TO RECOGNIZE RAGE?

Beyond the obvious reasons that feeling angry is unpleasant and that anger in others causes distress, general angry behavior in our modern world is unproductive and interferes with basic human interaction, communication, and performance. Anger, which evolved to ensure fair distribution of resources, residence, and relationships, can actually impede our successful accumulation of them all.

From a personal, psychological viewpoint, anger can make *you* a casualty. Studies show that it can take hours and even days for a person to calm down after a heated exchange. We have the tendency to mull over strong negative incidents, not allowing the emotion to dissipate, rather than doing just the opposite—using our PFC to consciously let go of the emotion and change our mind-set. We become the victim of our anger instead of the person at whom it was intended. Buddha had it right when he said, "Holding on to anger is like grasping a hot coal with the intent of throwing it at someone else; you are the one getting burned."

The same is true when you react angrily to someone else's anger charge. The emotion of anger can be like a heavy weight dangling around your neck, getting in the way of your peace of mind and your ability to think clearly, communicate effectively, and experience happier emotions.

A more insidious price of anger is isolation. Remember, there is an alternative to "fight," and that is "flight." This is an avoidance behavior exercised by a person who has no interest in changing the angry person's behavior; she just wants to get away from the potential danger as fast as she can.

The angry person may think he has won, driving away the person whose behavior he wanted to change. However, this does not really mean that the other person has done what the angry person wants, just that she has gone away. The oft-unintended consequence of anger is being alone. Anger can drive people away. How many times have you been in an argument with someone and he walks out? It doesn't make you feel any better. The reward of your victory is loneliness. And in an ironic twist, being lonely can make you even angrier. Human beings are designed to live in small groups for protection. When isolated, you can become more anxious, as you are more vulnerable. But one way to ward off threats is to activate your own threat display, anger. You will be safer, perhaps, but all alone.

HOW WE CONTROL ANGER

As we get older, we often become more able to recognize our rage and develop more efficient ways of managing the anger we feel. But the anger response itself doesn't change. It frequently results from the same types of things we experienced as kids, such as being criticized or threatened, just in an adult form. The three domains are always in existence. Whether it's my bowl of Cheerios or my credit card number you're trying to steal, the resulting emotion will be the same. In the following story of Joanna, the only top female executive in her firm, we can see how she experienced searing rage, but was able to control it appropriately.

Joanna was told that half her division would have to be laid off, a strategic decision on which she was never consulted but felt she should have been. She politely suggested that the decision be reconsidered, as she had supporting data that could affect the decision, but was denied. After the meeting, Joanna returned to her desk and typed her letter of resignation. She phoned her lawyer and then her husband, then she wept. Afterward, she hit the delete button on the letter of resignation.

It wasn't the cutbacks that angered Joanna; rather, it was that her opinion was not considered. She had been dismissed as unimportant and not shown any respect. Her domain of residence, her workplace, had been threatened. Her resources were being cut: half her division was being laid off. And her relationships, not only in her division but between her and the rest of the management team, had been threatened by the disregard for her input. Not only was this an affront and insult now, but she also wondered what it boded for the future. She felt as if she had been cast from the in-group and into an out-group.

Despite her shock and rage, she suppressed the urge to lash out during the meeting, knowing it would not reverse any decisions and might jeopardize her position. Instead, she wrote the letter of resignation and sought professional advice and moral support. She reached out to people she trusted to vent her emotions, to people where her value was unquestioned. In exercising these harmless but effective measures and evaluating her options, Joanna was recognizing her rage, whether she was conscious of it or not.

Joanne demonstrated what most of us do every day. Despite her urges, she controlled them, channeled them, and kept her cool. This amazing example of cortical control is no doubt what kept her job. If anger is an emotion designed to change the behavior of someone else, Joanne was smart not to show her frustration. The decision had already been made, and no amount of anger was going to change it. But she found a way to express it safely, then continue in her work.

Another way to think about Joanne's anger is to put it in the context of time—not just how quickly she got angry but also how long she held on to it. In the scenario I've described, there was a sudden anger trigger. But in a relatively short period of time, Joanna accepted the circumstances. She recognized that it was not a personal decision on the part of management for her unit to be laid off. This was a corporation focused on the bottom line. And she realized that she could not change the situation by responding angrily, so her motivation then became to protect her own position. Intense as her anger may have been, she used her ability to think things through—such PFC functions as *recognizing* and *realizing*—to defuse her own limbic anger. She used her modern brain to outsmart her ancient dangerous emotion.

Contrast that to someone who has gone through a difficult marriage and a more difficult divorce and has developed seething anger that festers—the kind that leads to screaming matches when the kids get picked up, or even to the need for restraining orders. I have seen this type of anger last for years, even a lifetime. When this kind of anger goes unrecognized, it can lead to significant difficulty both for internal health and external relationships. This is why it's crucial, especially when children are involved, to handle emotions in an adult way. Professional help is widely available, and many management techniques, support groups, and even self-help books are easily accessible to people with difficulty processing anger. One woman I know used humor to outsmart anger regarding her particularly acrimonious divorce. In session she once said, "I'm a divorcee, but always wanted to be a widow."

Exercise: Anger Versus Your PFC

The control of anger rests in our PFC, the thinking part of our brain. Two important neocortical functions are language and math, and here you'll use both to exercise your PFC. Let's look at language first. Think about the wide range of words we use for the various degrees of anger we can experience: irritation, fury, vexation, annoyance, frustration, anger, impatience, aggravation, displeasure, disgust. Of course, anger has many other creative names, including pissed, heated, ballistic, postal, ticked.

A simple self-help exercise you can do to begin to outsmart your anger is to construct your own personal anger scale. Feel free to use some of these words and any others you come up with. Once you have your list of ten words, assign each a number according to its intensity for you. My own personal scale from 1 to 10 (10 being the angriest) is irritation, aggravation, annoyance, frustration, impatience, displeasure, anger, wrath, fury, and rage. In creating this numbered word scale, we combine language and math, firmly shifting the nexus of control to the PFC.

Recognition itself is a thinking task, and it is important to recognize these nuances of anger. We experience levels 1 to 5 on my scale as human beings every day. But be wary if your anger burns into the range of 6 and above. Anger that shifts beyond 6 carries a much higher risk of true conflict, of verbal fights and aggression, and even of physical violence. Above 5, your limbic system begins to overwhelm your PFC. By keeping yourself below a 5, you can normally use your cortical control and keep your anger under

(continued)

wraps. Recognition, in essence "re-cognition," keeps your PFC well exercised while also *exorcizing* your limbic "logic" that tells you to just fight and get it over with. With this exercise, you are shifting the locus of control from the limbic system to the PFC, exactly where you want to be to outsmart your anger.

You have a lot to lose when you're not able to recognize rage. In Joanna's case, she could have lost her job. But unrecognized rage can lead to loss of resources, residence, relationships, opportunities, respect from peers, and much more.

Now that you have placed your word list on a 1–10 scale, write down some of the triggers of your limbic response. Go through this list and give each item a word and number from your anger response scale. Include them next to the example in parentheses. Here are some of my triggers and responses as examples:

Burning a piece of toast (1, irritation)

Slow Internet connection (3, annoyance)

Bad cell phone range (2, aggravation)

Crime in the neighborhood (7, anger)

Disrespectful boss (7, anger)

Scratch on your car (6, displeasure)

Cheating spouse (8, wrath . . . but, thankfully, this has never happened!)

Here are others for you to complete:

Annoying cell phone ring tones

Missing your train or bus

Crying baby on airplane

Neighbor child being mean to your child

Critical in-laws

Rude store clerk

Whining from your kids

Running out of gas

Not getting a raise

Getting cut off by another driver

You may find that some of these overlap, with more than one selection hovering at a 3 or 4 and none of these choices reaching the threshold of a 9 or 10. But I encourage you to delve deeper into yourself and find your 8s, 9s, and 10s. They may be hard to admit. Encourage your friends, family, and coworkers to make their own lists and compare notes. At home, perhaps spend time at dinner talking about them. At work, if you are a boss, give your employees some time to make and share their lists. The more you know about what makes one another angry, the better the chance of either avoiding those triggers or being able to understand and manage them should they occur. Families can become closer, relationships can become stronger, and the workplace can become more productive when we know how to outsmart anger.

Finally it is time to place your list items within the framework of the three domains: food (resources), shelter (residence), or mate (relationships). For example, thinking about all the repairs that need work in your house would probably go in the residence category. Burning a piece of toast wastes time and food, both resources. Of course, sometimes the causes of anger overlap. If you were making that toast for your partner, perhaps you worry that the relationship will be jeopardized. (But if your relationship is so fragile that burning a piece of toast could put it in danger, you may want to think about the relationship itself!)

Your list will look something like this when you are finished (although you are never *really* finished, as you can always add something new to the list should it occur):

(*continued*)

Burning a piece of toast (1, irritation, resource)

Slow Internet connection (3, annoyance, resource)

Bad cell phone range (2, aggravation, resource)

Crime in the neighborhood (7, anger, residence)

Disrespectful boss (7, anger, relationship)

Scratch on your car (6, displeasure, resource)

Cheating spouse (8, wrath, relationship . . . but, thankfully, this still has never happened!)

What needs to change in one of the domains, be it resources, residence, or relationships, to move you from a 5 to a 3, or make you less angry? What about from a 5 to a 7, making you angrier? What becomes evident as you recognize what irritates you is that you actually have a lot of control over your anger. These differences are clues about what needs to change for you to be calmer and less likely to escalate to the more intense feelings of anger. The more control you have, the less anxious you will be and also the less likely you will be to get angry in response to a world that now seems less threatening. Keep these lists. We will be referring to them throughout the book.

THE PFC IN ACTION: WHAT YOU THINK AFFECTS WHAT YOU FEEL

Are you someone who thinks that "human civilization" is an oxymoron? Or do you have eternal faith in your fellow man? Your underlying worldview and feelings about people, even your sporadic moods, impact how you interpret the world around you from moment to moment.

You know this from your own experience. When things are going great and you're feeling relaxed, you are not going to jump to anger as quickly as when you are feeling stressed and have many pressures on you at once. Feeling relaxed is a mind-set that allows the PFC to operate at maximum capacity and filter the emotions that automatically spring into the brain. Someone who exercises or meditates a lot may feel and behave quite differently in regard to a threat to a domain than someone who was raised in a war-torn country where resources were scarce or in a neighborhood where crime was just outside the door or in a family where duress and conflict were more the norm than love, support, safety, and respect.

This has been shown to be particularly true in the case of fear, which correlates closely to anger. Scientists at the University of Hull in Britain wanted to know whether or not a fearful mind-set increased the likelihood of a fear-based reaction to a threat. The researchers showed volunteers a sequence of computer images—some threatening, some neutral—over varying blocks of time. The results showed that volunteers who expected something bad to happen were more likely to overestimate threat and express more fear. They perceived events differently than the people who didn't have negative, fear-based expectations.

These are important results that can be extrapolated to anger. The way we feel has an effect on the way we think, just as what we think affects what we feel. If we are walking around with an angry brain, we may misperceive the cues of the world around us and project our own anger onto what could be much more benign and neutral stimuli. Our anger pump has been primed, and we may see anger and threats where none exist.

In my profession we call this phenomenon "projection." Just like a movie that is projected onto a screen, we project the way we feel onto others, imagining they feel the same way. So if I feel angry, then everyone feels angry. If I don't like myself, then I imagine no one likes me. In a way, this leads to a self-fulfilling prophecy in which we create the very thing we fear the most. I believe that anger works the same way. Anger keeps other people away from us, but on some level it is this loneliness that we fear the most. If we are angry and threatening, is it any surprise we may feel more isolated, leading us to feel ostracized, which then leads to more anger? Recognizing that you are angry is the first step in understanding what has happened in your world to make you feel that way. When you are able to do this, you will be able to recognize what makes others angry as well.

Being able to accurately recognize your own rage, in all its forms and nuances, is incredibly important. When we can recognize our own feelings, we have a better chance of more accurately recognizing the feelings of others. This ability creates much more clarity when interacting with others, and clarity in communication decreases the chances of misunderstandings and therefore anger and potential aggression.

RECOGNIZING RAGE IN OTHERS

Being able to recognize your own rage can have enormous benefits for your mood and productivity. But it also can help you recognize what triggers anger in others. One simple reason is that we have all evolved basically the same brain. If I get angry about something, chances are good that you will get angry about something similar. So if I want to avoid a potential conflict with you, I need not only to know which of your resources, residence, or relationships you think I may be threatening but also to be able to recognize by your face and body that you are getting heated. From a simple survival point of view, recognizing rage in others is a good thing to do.

Using my PFC, I can anticipate the consequence of an action. For example, if I take your candy bar or mate, it would be good for me to anticipate the consequence: you are probably going to try to stop me and even bop me. I want to be able to judge from your face and body how you will respond. The red face of anger is just like any other warning sign designed to signal danger.

You can see the veins in some people's necks or foreheads stand out when they get angry, a signal that their blood pressure is going up. In some people you can see their muscles tense, another visual cue that they are mobilizing the strength they may need to protect their stuff and change your approach. Hundreds of thousands of years ago, we developed and used these signals to choose either to attack or to retreat, in the limbic days of our ancestors.

In our modern age, most of us have become very adept at recognizing anger in others, but we aren't born this way. Identifying anger, as well as other human signals and emotions, requires years of brain "programming," most of which we don't even realize is happening.

Infants are good at detecting threats, such as unfamiliar faces, and expressing anger, but not always so good at detecting anger in other people. That ability develops later, around the age of three. In order for a child to identify that someone else is having an internal experience, at least two things have to happen. First, a child has to distinguish between herself and other people. Babies are not born with this ability. Have you ever been to a newborn nursery? When one baby cries, they all may start crying. For these babies, who are without awareness that they are separate individuals, the cry they hear may very well be their own, so they start crying themselves.

This realization of being a separate entity occurs around the age of eighteen months, and sets the stage for the development of ToM, the ability to appreciate someone else's thoughts and feelings. Once this happens, an infant's brain begins building the foundation of a most critical component of being human, empathy. Empathy is the ability to appreciate what someone else is thinking or feeling and then to let that person *know* you have a sense of what he is thinking and feeling, of what he is experiencing in life.

When a toddler approaches his mother with a Band-Aid or kiss when she has a "boo-boo," this action implies that the child both distinguished himself from the mother and recognized the mother's internal experience of distress, likely connecting it to a memory of a time he himself got a boo-boo and what his mother did in response. A child with this ability has a growing awareness that a particular shape of the face is the visual expression of a hidden, invisible, internal emotion.

The ability to distinguish an angry face is fairly well developed by the time a child is ready to enter kindergarten. The brain of a five- or six-year-old has already experienced and begun to categorize nuances in thousands of facial expressions, but from a relatively limited number of faces. At this age, children have connected the face with a perception of the internal experience of the person who is making the face. At the age of six, they are pretty good at knowing Mommy's angry face, Daddy's angry face, and those of brother James and sister Sue. That the angry face has a relatively consistent geometry among people is comforting, but now children are thrust into a larger social network, school, and have to generalize their home-based knowledge to a world of strangers. They will need to learn to cooperate or compete, and being able to connect the external clues of another kid's face with what that kid may be thinking or feeling is an enormous task indeed. But they do it.

WHEN YOU RECOGNIZE ANOTHER'S RAGE, IT HELPS EVERYONE

By the time a child is nine, the ability to recognize rage in others is as solid as it is in most adults. But another component has been added: the carryover of one experience to another. How we perceive another person is influenced by our earlier experiences, and not always of the same person. The next time Billy plays a game with someone other than Jenny, he may be more vigilant about the possibility of her cheating. Our highly developed human memory allows us to do this: we carry with us our previous experiences to the next social interaction. Memory is a limbic system responsibility, but how we act on those memories shifts to the PFC, influenced by those limbic remembrances.

Although this ability can be useful in protecting us from being cheated, it can also have the opposite effect: another person's negative behaviors can prime you for anger. When people are constantly primed for anger by others' behaviors, they are likely to respond more easily to triggers and behave more angrily toward others. Just as happiness is contagious, so is anger. Until someone breaks the cycle.

That someone can be you. So even as you recognize your own range of anger responses, you have to realize that you can ease the anger of others, or increase it, by the way you influence the other person's perception of you. If you're in anger mode, you trigger the anger mode in someone else. Sound familiar? How you treat others has an impact on whether you feel empowered, valued, and recognized, or angry, frustrated, and alone. The Rolling Stones had it right in the lyrics of their 1969 smash hit "Let It Bleed": We all need someone we can lean on. The lessons learned here are applicable to pretty much all human interaction. A warm, genuine, accessible person who helps other people feel accepted and comfortable is more likely to disarm the force of anger in those people.

In this chapter, we have explored how to recognize rage in ourselves and in others, and why doing so is important. In the next two chapters, we will look closely at how basic behavioral components lead to thoughts and then to feelings of anger. Human beings are hardwired to feel anger as a way to protect ourselves against a perceived threat: our anger is designed either to drive the threat away by inducing fear or to mobilize our brain and body to fight that threat directly and get it to go away.

In this chapter, we have learned how to recognize rage. But how do we tame this most dangerous emotion? To do this we must first understand what those things are that get us angry to begin with. Look at the list you made. It will serve as a guide as we begin to explore why we mobilize our powerful experience of anger.

CHAPTER 3

Envision Envy

Hatred is active, and envy passive dislike;
there is but one step from envy to hate.
—Johann Wolfgang von Goethe (1749–1832)

Upon graduation from college, grammar school buddies Ronald and Kurt were commissioned as officers in the U.S. Army, pinning onto their uniforms each other's gold bars. Their careers followed similar paths, each exhibiting exemplary leadership qualities in both command and staff assignments, resulting in glowing efficiency reports. Ronald and Kurt held coveted infantry command positions when their individual performance records were submitted to the selection board for potential promotion to the next rank. As fate and the military selection process would have it, Kurt was tapped for promotion and Ronald was not. As Ronald pinned upon Kurt's uniform the silver eagles designating the rank of colonel, he felt happy for his old friend, but inside he felt a profound hurt when he saw the shining eagles on Kurt's uniform and not his.

ENVY: A CLOSE FRIEND OF ANGER

When Ronald thought deeply about whether or not he wanted his childhood buddy to be promoted, there wasn't even a question. Such an acknowledgment would be a source of pride for everyone back home. He truly loved and supported his friend, like a brother. But in that first moment, as he saw the shine of the eagles and the smile on

Kurt's face, his automatic emotional response—the part he had no control over—was to wish that he, not Kurt, had been promoted to colonel.

This familiar scenario is simply a modern-day manifestation of the biblical concept of envy. Long considered one of the Seven Deadly Sins in both Christianity and Judaism, envy has been with us as long as humankind has been keeping track of the ills of the heart and mind. And these days, envy is not just alive and kicking—it's flourishing.

In fact, envy has festered into one of our greatest sources of anger, especially in our current materialistic culture where symbols of wealth like fancy cars and jewelry (even the fake stuff) are flaunted with reckless abandon. For many people who feel that they too deserve the spoils of wealth, these constant reminders of what they don't have often leads to resentment and anger. In my twenty-plus years of experience as a psychiatrist, I have seen the desire to "get" the things they envy drive people to lose sight of the most important values in their lives. We feel envious of friends, total strangers, TV characters, classmates, or colleagues. We often feel the deepest envy toward those closest to us, as in Ronald's case.

Although we could view Ronald as duplicitous and insincere, his feelings were completely normal. We are complicated and multifaceted beings, and envy is as much a part of who we are as feelings of joy, sadness, and anger itself. The way to defeat the negative feeling of envy is to learn how to recognize and handle it when it sneaks up on you and to cut it off at the pass—clearly, no easy feat.

Learning to envision envy is critical to leading a happier, less conflict-driven, less angry life. When even the smallest infraction— for example, "He got a bigger piece of cake than I did" (from adults, mind you!)—leads to an emotional meltdown and lasting resentment, it's time to develop an awareness of envy's relationship to anger and learn how to change your perspective from "get" to "give." In doing so, you can help shift your internal compass from "me" to the broader and more productive "we," reducing tension and pent-up feelings of anger between people, whether they're strangers, close friends, or even siblings. It is time to transform from the "Me" generation to the "We" generation to help us live calmer, safer, and happier lives.

UNDERSTANDING ENVY

Envy is that unpleasant, often painful feeling brought on by the good fortune of others. That good fortune could be just about anything—a beautiful possession, a great job, a new home, or a happy relationship. We see something we want, and we feel envy that someone else has it and we do not. Inside we might secretly wish that the other guy didn't have it or would lose it. Envy stems directly from our limbic reaction to the domains of resources, residence, and relationships; you don't have enough while someone else has more. Envy is sneaky and manipulative, but whether it's a twinge or an ache, we all feel it. There is always someone richer than we are, faster than we are, more beautiful or youthful, and *we want what he or she has*. Someone always has a better house or a safer community. Someone always seems to have a hotter boyfriend or girlfriend, a better boss, or a better relationship whatever the type. When we experience envy, we resent that another person has something that we feel we lack. The true pain is caused when the mind focuses on what one desires but cannot have.

GREEN-EYED MONSTER OR GREEN WITH ENVY?

Oftentimes people use the terms *jealousy* and *envy* interchangeably, but the two are actually distinct emotional cousins. With malicious envy, you believe in your heart of hearts that you will *never* be able to get what someone else has. The emotion is less focused on the individual than on the resource or the success. For instance, a teen might say, "Why does my friend Jennifer

(continued)

get to wear the expensive jeans?!!" You don't necessarily feel anger or hatred toward that individual because she has more; you just feel bad because *you* don't have it. Uncontrolled envy like this can turn into what *seems* like a jealous rage. Take the Snow White fairy tale. The evil stepmother envies poor Snow White's beauty. Her obsessive vendetta against Snow White has only to do with what she wants and cannot get. Her tragic solution, as we all know, is to knock off the young beauty with a poisoned apple.

Jealousy, in contrast, cuts right to the fear of loss, particularly within the domain of relationships. It is the wish to keep what you have that someone else could take from you. If you are the jealous type, you might become uneasy when you hear that your new boyfriend was seen with another woman. That woman might in fact be his sister or colleague, but the jealous mind can quickly jump to the dark, angry possibility of a rival. You can also be jealous of your colleague because the boss gives him more attention. A salient example of jealousy run amok is in Shakespeare's tragedy *Othello*, in which the term *green-eyed monster* was first penned. The evil Iago (envious of Othello's position) plots to make it appear as if Othello's wife, Desdemona, is having an affair with Cassio. Confronted with what he thinks is "proof," Othello flies into a jealous rage and smothers his beloved Desdemona. Jealousy may lead to suspicion, another source of anger, which we explore in the next chapter.

It's easy to see why envy and jealousy get mixed up. These are both feelings that bring up deep insecurities and anxiety in people—lack of resources and loss of relationships. And envy and jealousy are commonly experienced together—another reason for their confusion. You can be envious of another guy's wealth and status, and become jealous when he starts flirting with your wife. Each is capable of sparking hurt, anger, and aggression.

THE TWO FACES OF ENVY

Rather than delve one-sidedly into the typically dark world of envy—"malicious envy" (wanting something bad to happen to the person you envy)—it's important to note that unlike the other cardinal sins, envy does have a potentially positive side. Just as anger has a good side—it once protected us from predators—or can be channeled to good use (such as by pushing for safe driving laws because someone cut you off while he was texting, for example), envy can sometimes be the force that motivates us to strive harder. If I envy my neighbor's new, shiny, red Lamborghini, it might get me to thinking that if I saved some money and worked extra hard for a bonus this year, that vehicle could be sitting in my driveway too. Sometimes envy serves as incentive. In this case, it's called "benign envy," something that few people have ever heard of but that we all have experienced.

Indeed, in most languages, there is just the one word for envy, and most people think of it immediately as the malicious sort. But the Dutch have a specific word for benign envy, *benigjden*, which might explain why some very interesting research on envy is coming from the Netherlands these days. Researchers at Tilburg University have been looking deeply at the motivations behind both benign and malicious envy and have discovered that benign envy may be particularly useful in motivating people to work harder.

In one insightful experiment, Niels van de Ven and his team of Tilburg researchers split a group of college students into two categories. The first was prepped to think that "behavior change is easy" and was given a story to read about a man who overcame many obstacles to become a famous scientist. The other group was encouraged to think that "behavior change was hard" and heard a slightly different version of the story; this time the man was always on track to being a great scientist and ultimately became famous. Both groups were then given the same newspaper article about an outstanding student who did well in a national academic competition.

After reading this article, participants were asked to rate how much they felt benign envy (wanting to be like this student), admiration (appreciating the student's accomplishment), or malicious envy (wanting the student to fail). Last, the students were asked to estimate how many more hours they planned to study in the next academic semester.

The study results showed that the "behavior change is easy" participants were more likely to feel benign envy toward the excellent student. The "behavior change is hard" group was more likely to feel admiration. Both groups had the same number of people who reported malicious envy. But what really surprised the researchers was what they found when they looked at the estimated hours the students planned to study. The benign envy group planned to study longer hours than the admiration group. This is important stuff. If you believe that improvement and success are under your own control, you will experience more benign envy, which leads to increased motivation to work harder. But when you think improvement is out of your control, you may feel admiration for the successful person, but do not become motivated to try. Why bother wasting your energy if success is not an option?

Other studies by this Dutch team found that the feeling of benign envy led to a comparing of oneself "up," the proverbial "keeping up with the Joneses" mentality, as opposed to the comparing of oneself "down," which usually comes with malicious envy. You experience malicious envy when you have no confidence in yourself to ever attain the same resources, residence, or relationships that the envied person has. You experience benign envy when you know you can have what another person has if you just strive hard enough.

These observations led to some surprising insights into how both benign and malicious envy can even affect consumer behavior. Dr. van de Ven's team found that people who experienced benign envy were willing to spend more money on certain products. Researchers asked college students to read a short story with a color image of an iPhone at the top. Then they were asked to imagine working with a fellow student on a project. This student had an iPhone and showed them some of its many features. As in the previous study, these students were randomly assigned to different mind-set conditions—benign envy, malicious envy, or control (noncondi- tioned) groupings.

The results this time showed the tendency of those with benign envy to compare "up," and in this case, benign envy motivated them to spend more money. "Our studies showed that people who had been made envious of someone who owned an iPhone were willing to pay 80 Euros more on average," wrote the authors, van de Ven, Zeelenberg, and Pieters. But this occurred only for those who expe- rienced benign envy and who believed the person who owned the iPhone, a student like them, was presumably deserving of it.

Among those students who were conditioned with malicious envy, something very different occurred. Although they too were willing to pay more, they were not willing to pay more for the same product they envied. Instead, this group was more likely to buy a competing product, a BlackBerry. The bottom line: if someone who has some- thing appears undeserving of it, the response to this person will most likely be malicious envy—driving people away from products. "Adver- tisers should make sure that the celebrities they want to use in their ads actually deserve their status," the authors wrote in their study. "If they do not, these celebrities might actually trigger malicious envy and the sales of products from a competitor could even go up." Some- times we do the opposite of what the very people we envy the most might do. Because we know we cannot be like them, we pretend to have some control and choose not to be like them.

Both benignly and maliciously envious people feel frustrated. These are equally intense and negative experiences, and both drive people to seek to level the playing field—one by pulling themselves up and the other by pulling another person down. But surprisingly, both of these sensations occur within the very same place in the brain.

THE BRAIN ON ENVY

By the age of four months, a baby begins to compare bits of information. The infant cries when she sees a stranger's face because it's different than her mother's. When it comes to envy, the same mechanism is at play. We compare bits of information about others to ourselves, and when we feel that we do not compare well, we feel unhappy and often angry. It is only in this comparison that we can experience envy. This is an important observation. We feel at a disadvantage, which leads us to feel threatened, which in turn means that we have to either run away for safety or attack in anger.

Although humans have cooperated to the extent that the species has more than survived, we are still at risk—on a deep, limbic brain level—of rarely feeling satisfied or full up. This is a brutal truth about how we have evolved as human beings. Perhaps one of the obvious reasons envy developed stems from our ancestors' early days when the acquisition of resources—mainly food—may have meant the difference between life and death. One would have noticed when another had more of something. If you had something I wanted or needed that put you at a survival advantage over me, I might try to take it from you. But if you are already at an advantage, I probably wouldn't be able to just step in and take it. You might be stronger, smarter, perhaps more overtly resourceful. I would have to be covertly resourceful and plan my actions for the future.

This planning is a PFC function. Envy filtered through the PFC would enable us to assess a situation and plan a response, which in turn enhanced our survival potential. It is a lot more effective than being impulsive. As kids we are taught to look both ways before crossing a street: an exercise in assessing the relative danger of our surroundings, making a plan based on that assessment, and anticipating the outcome. Only then do we actually take the action of crossing the street. Kids need to be taught these basic survival tools because the child and adolescent brain is an impulsive brain, with a relatively immature PFC compared to the limbic system, which is the location of impulsivity. Even as this limbic system may harbor the emotion of envy, it depends on the PFC to elaborate and execute the plan to level the playing field or, better, to jump up a level so that you are now the one being envied.

The two types of envy, benign and malicious, both push a person to strive either for personal success in healthy competition or to bring the other person down in unhealthy aggression that can lead to war. From an evolutionary perspective, envy is yet another means of survival—of getting more resources, residence, or relationships—driving humans not only to have more but also to deprive the other of those same means of survival.

THE PAIN OF ENVY

After six million years of evolution, envy is hardwired in the brain. Using the advanced imaging provided by fMRI technology, neuroscientists have even been able to trace precisely where in the brain envy lives: in the limbic system. Recently, researchers at the University of Haifa studied fMRI scans of volunteers who were primed with envy-provoking situations. In each scan, envy activated the part of the brain that bridges limbic structures (such as the amygdalae, hippocampus, and midline thalamus) to certain regions of the PFC.

Neuroscientists at the National Institute of Radiological Sciences in Japan conducted similar brain scans of study volunteers who were told to imagine themselves in situations where they had either greater or lesser status. They too isolated the brain activity to the ventral striatum. But they also discovered something else. When the participants discussed someone they envied, the pain nodes in the anterior cingulate cortex lit up. The more they envied the person, the more the pain. This section of the brain is also associated with conflict and is activated during sensations of both physical and emotional pain—specifically pain associated with social exclusion. No surprise here: envy really hurts.

At the same time, the researchers were also able to see what happened in the brain when something negative befell the envied person. This time the participants read a story in which the one on the pedestal suffered various misfortunes, including a bout of food poisoning. When the hard luck happened, the brain's reward reaction section lit up—the very same thing that happens when a person receives good fortune. Lead author Dr. Hidehiko Takahashi summarized the results of their study with an old Japanese expression. "The misfortunes of others are the taste of honey," he said. "The ventral striatum is processing that 'honey.'"

These connections suggest that although the emotion of envy is harbored in the primitive limbic system, the limbic system is then signaling the more modern PFC. It is as if the limbic system shouts out, "Hey PFC. That guy has a red Ferrari and I want it. What's going on? Please assess this situation." The PFC does its job, observing that the person has more resources than you and relaying that back to the limbic system. This comparison can activate a desire to change those findings. "Hey PFC, what can we do about this?" asks the limbic system. After another analysis, the PFC sends back the daunting news that nothing can be done. That is when the limbic system activates envy: you are at a serious disadvantage and can do nothing. At least not yet.

Envy is interesting because unlike many other emotions, it intrinsically calls for PFC assessment. Frequently people are unaware of exactly how they feel about something. But envy requires a response from the PFC. The limbic system sends the message, "Hey PFC, keep your thoughts open for an opportunity to get even. Your job is to make a plan, take an action, and anticipate the consequence of that action."

Envy can lead to sustained and careful planning not just of how to get the desired object, as in benign envy, but also of how to get even with the person who does have it. Revenge driven by envy is all too common in our society. The activation of pain receptors keeps the PFC alert to an opportunity to change, and if the change can't include getting what you want, then it might be pleasant to think about all

THE ALLURE OF ENVY

For all there is to dislike about our envious ways, the flip side is that many people enjoy being envied. Why? Being envied can be good for your self-confidence: it's nice to know you have something that another person wants, especially if you are not in any danger of having it taken from you. We have all seen humans' capacity for gloating: think of when your sister showed off her new phone or when a neighbor came over driving a new convertible. If you do not seem a bit envious, you can almost see the disappointment in their faces. But watch them beam when you say how envious you are and how you wish you could try out the phone or take the car for at least one drive.

These observations of our human nature were confirmed by a study done by researchers at Wesleyan University who took two different cultural groups, Hispanic American and European American, and surveyed their emotions throughout various envy scenarios. Interestingly, being envied had both more positive and more negative psychological significance among those participants who were achievement oriented (European Americans) than among participants who considered themselves more oriented to "cooperation and interpersonal harmony"— the Hispanic group. Although envy itself appears to be universal, there may indeed be cultural attitudes that protect certain groups from the high levels of distress caused by this potentially rogue emotion.

the bad things that could happen to the person you envy. This delayed gratification was exquisitely captured by the French novelist Marie Joseph Eugène Sue, who wrote in his 1841 book *Mathilde*, "Revenge is a dish best served cold." Wait until your object of envy has forgotten how injured you feel—and then strike. But this final plan motivated by envy is not always the wisest course of action. What a waste of a brain so adept at planning.

THE UNUSUAL PLEASURE OF ENVY: SCHADENFREUDE

I recently saw a Broadway show I really liked, called *Avenue Q*. I bring it up here because one of the numbers in the show is about this very pleasure we take in others' misfortune. Another word for this pleasure, and the title of the song, is "Schadenfreude," which comes from the German words *Schaden* and *Freude*, "harm" and "joy." Seeing a puppet and an actor sing this song allows the audience to laugh unabashedly at our constant human folly. In the song, the characters acknowledge their enjoyment at seeing waitresses dropping a tray of glasses, figure skaters falling on their asses, feeling happy that someone else is feeling crappy, and other insights into this unusual side of all of us.

As one of the characters says, schadenfreude is part of "human nature," and goes on to say how glad we can be at times that "I'm not you." In fact, a phrase like this has made its way into our culture rife with its negative connotation: "It must suck to be you." Putting this concept into a song not only highlights the brilliance of the writers, Robert Lopez, Jeff Marx, and Jeff Whitty, but shines the light of insight on all of us. It is a song that most of the audience relates to, myself included, demonstrated by the tear-producing laughter it elicits. Schadenfreude is felt so universally. We cannot help but bask in delight when certain people, especially certain popular celebrities, politicians, and other public figures, make embarrassing mistakes.

But studies have shown that we experience much higher levels of pleasure when the person we envy is a peer. The closer the person is to us in stature, the more we envy him and the more pleasure we experience at his expense, such as when an overpaid colleague gets fired from the company. Australian psychiatrist Norman Feather studies this group of envied people among us, whom he calls "tall poppies." In fact, the social phenomenon called tall poppy syndrome, known more widely in other English-speaking parts of the world, is demonstrated by those engaging in the practice of cutting down or criticizing other people because their talents or achievements elevate them above their peers. Quite different from envying Hollywood celebrities from afar.

From an evolutionary standpoint, schadenfreude as a natural extension of envy would of course make sense. If there were but one banana on the tree, I'd have a better chance of getting it if my competition slipped off the branch, so seeing this happen to someone who has advantages over me (perhaps he is better and faster at climbing trees) would give me pleasure. If that competitor were my kid, however, or someone in whom I was invested, I would either get down and help him or share the prize when won.

The dilemma we face when we envision envy is that we do not live in a world where bananas, or many other necessary items, are a limited resource. Our limbic brain has not kept up with the rapid development of our civilization and technology. What was once an imperative for survival has become an obstacle for the greater global survival of a species whose members are so intimately interconnected. Malicious envy and schadenfreude are emotions that are simply not helping advance our species, let alone our closest relationships. Rather, they arrest our development, perpetuate division and prejudice, and keep us limited to the primitive jungle of our limbic brain.

ENVY'S IMPACT ON YOU

You may have heard the fable of the envious eagle. One eagle is a strong and fast flyer; the other, motivated by envy, removes his own feather to try to shoot the stronger eagle down. He fails, and so plucks another feather and then another, until he can no longer fly at all.

What is clear is that when we allow ourselves to fall prey to the lure of envy, it can cost us dearly. The feeling of envy brought about by the process of comparison can seriously impede a person's progress in life. When you compare yourself down, you are choosing to highlight what you perceive as your weakness rather than focus on your strength. Research has shown that those who are most envious, and especially susceptible to schadenfreude, are the same people who have the lowest levels of self-esteem.

But beyond self-esteem, envy also inhibits brain performance. In a recent study by psychology researchers from Texas Christian University, subjects showed increased memory of detail regarding the person being envied, but were less able to self-regulate and attend to their own current tasks. What this means for everyone is that rather than living in the moment we have, we live in the moments we wish we had, at enormous expense and sacrifice of satisfaction. Distracted by its built-in propensity to compare things, your own brain turns against you. Envy robs you of your ability to manage the basic tasks essential for success in your daily life. Ruminating and wishing you had what your neighbor has can take away your joy at home. At work, envy can become such a distracter that your boss may notice, making it even more difficult to advance your career, and potentially widening the very gap that you fear exists between yourself and the object of your envy. If there were ever a recipe for failure in life, envy would be the first ingredient.

ENVY AND OTHERS: CREATING RIVALS

Envy can also wreak havoc by creating rifts between people and even rifts between groups. Here's one example I like to cite because it resonates with me personally, and anyone who loves a favorite local team will understand. Sports fans across the world know about rivalries. We choose a group to favor over another, be it a soccer, cricket, rugby, football, or hockey team. It can be a professional team or a school rivalry. For me, it's the Boston Red Sox. And any Red Sox fan is almost required to hate our biggest rival: the New York Yankees.

As an ardent Red Sox fan, I used to hate the Yankees as well. Why? Because they always won, and they did not seem particularly humble or sportsmanlike about it. What made it worse was that to the Yankee fans I knew (yes, I actually have friends who are Yankee fans), the "rivalry" did not seem that important to them. In fact, they didn't even acknowledge the Red Sox or distinguish them from any other team. The highest regard one Yankee fan gave to the Red Sox was to say that they were the "best June team in baseball," meaning that when the wins didn't count—at the beginning of the season—the Sox were good, but under pressure they crumbled.

Whenever the Yankees lost, I felt great—typical schadenfreude. Difficult as it was to admit, I worried that the Red Sox were just not the Yankees. Now for most people this was a pretty harmless sort of schadenfreude. But you can see how attractive vengefulness can be when one is on the losing side of the bleachers. There is enormous relief from this sense of baseball inadequacy now that the Red Sox have gone on to win two World Series. My schadenfreude has decreased. Envy and hate have dissipated because I have what the Yankees had. Schadenfreude, the gloating you feel when a person you envy fails, reflects a feeling based on a sense of inferiority to begin with—of having less, being less, and fearing that one will always be less. Now that the Red Sox are consistent contenders, I would hope that we feel less schadenfreude when the Yankees lose, and just the simple enjoyment of good clean honest competition.

Envy of a sports team may be relatively benign, but other smaller actions are also inherently dangerous to humans, specifically lying. Recently, researchers at the University of North Carolina were looking into what compelled people to act dishonestly to help or hurt others. In two experiments, they randomly paired the study subjects and manipulated their wealth levels through a pretend lottery. The researchers then observed how disparity between partners influenced their behavior. What they found was that a perceived inequity of finances was a key condition that led to lying. When there is a perceived inequity, which can lead to envy, the person who has the short end of the stick may feel righteously justified in committing harmful acts, such as lying.

Another example of a small envy may be the teenager who is angry at having a curfew. The time limit represents parental power, of which some teens are envious. Rather than adhere to the limit, some may choose to flaunt that authority and break curfew, coming in late. Feeling disrespected, parents may in turn ground the child, attempting to reinforce the authoritarian hierarchy, which can potentially lead to another rebellion and the continuation of a cycle I see all too often in my psychiatry practice. These small envies can have long-lasting and detrimental effects on the entire family.

This book on anger cannot ignore the very significant angers present in the world today. Racial, socioeconomic, and gender divisions are central to envy, which can lead to hate and then to anger and aggression. We can tackle our own prejudices, but how do we address these larger social envies that lead to riots, intolerance, and war? These events hinge on the comparisons we make between each other as groups of human beings: haves versus have-nots, greedy versus lazy, a weaker out-group versus a powerful and resourceful in-group. For instance, the guiding slogan of the recent Occupy Wall Street movement, "We Are the 99%," focused squarely on the comparison between those who feel they have very little and the tiny fraction of those with the most.

When we're in comparison mode, we divide ourselves not only by envy but by our contempt toward other groups. Princeton psychologist Sarah Fiske discovered this when investigating how people think when making comparisons of their status against that of others. Her results, which she published as both a study and the book *Envy Up, Scorn Down: How Status Divides Us*, show how we perpetuate the racial and economic divides, the gender and age divisions, and the continued fractionalization of our society. For instance, the most envied groups in general included high-status people of any kind. They were viewed as competent but also cold—not warm or on "our" side and therefore untrustworthy. In the United States, according to Fiske, Asian and Jewish people are perceived this way, as well as female professionals. By contrast, the homeless and the very poor were viewed as neither competent nor warm, and in most societies, older people were widely viewed as incompetent. Even more disturbing was the finding that a person who looks down on another may also inhibit his or her own ToM. Scorn deactivates our interest in what other people think or feel, inhibits our empathy, and lays the foundation for dehumanization and the potential atrocities with which it is associated.

ACQUIRING MORE "STUFF" IS NOT AN ANTIDOTE TO ENVY

The fire of envy in our culture is fed each day by popular media and advertising. These messages are especially powerful among teens and highly impressionable young people. In our desire to fit in, to measure up, to be as good as that which we envy, we must consume. Even adults are urged, persuaded, and seduced by Madison Avenue slogans like Citibank's prerecession slogan, "Live Richly." Buying those designer jeans is the price of admission to being in the cool club.

We think that by consuming, we'll be the one who is envied. But keeping up with the Joneses will not only break your piggy bank but also inevitably fail to provide lasting joy.

Until recently, the connection between consumption and happiness was not well studied. Now researchers from British Columbia have found that consumers who spend money on an experience— concert tickets, a trip to Disney, a night on the town—wind up producing longer-lasting feelings of satisfaction than those who buy stuff. A similar investigation from the University of Wisconsin in Madison led by Dr. Thomas DeLeire that examined nine major categories of consumption showed that the only category positively related to happiness was leisure—vacations, entertainment, sports, and equipment like golf clubs and fishing poles. Still, many people buck this wisdom and convince themselves that "retail therapy" will improve their mood or increase their happiness. Too often what happens is that the dress that looked so good on your much-envied colleague doesn't look so great on you.

I had a patient who kept thinking that if only he had the latest smartphone or the newest computer or the latest pair of sneakers, he would finally feel accepted by his peers. Each new purchase provided short-lived satisfaction. As we explored his nearly obsessive drive to purchase companionship, he began to realize that what he really wanted was for someone to accept him for who he was, not for what he wore. In fact, his need to "out-Jones the Joneses" led to the impression that he was shallow and superficial, isolating him from the very relationships he so desperately desired.

Exercise: An Inventory of Envy

So how do you move beyond envy and arrive at a perspective from which you can appreciate what you have and obsess about what others have? One way to address envy is to create what I call an "inventory of envy."

Write down a list of items that you *think* you envy, such as your neighbor's new pool or your brother-in-law's new job. As you create your inventory, assign one of these words to each item:

Envy: a feeling of discontent or resentful longing provoked by someone else's possessions, qualities, or luck

Jealousy: fear of being replaced, of losing affection or position

Greed: an intense and selfish desire for something, such as wealth or power

Desire: a strong feeling of wanting to have something or wishing for something to happen

Coveting: yearning to possess or have something owned by someone else

Resentment: feeling deep and bitter anger and ill will

Grudge: a persistent feeling of ill will resulting from a past insult or injury

Materialism: a belief that material possessions and physical comfort are more important than spiritual values

Different situations may elicit different responses. For example, I may be jealous of a coworker but not resent her. However, I may resent my boss for appearing to give preferential treatment to my coworker. You may have other words you want to add to this list which describe your own personal feelings of envy. Being able to dissect the complexity of your envy will help you recognize that much of this emotion results in an enormous waste of energy that could be better spent achieving or acquiring the very things that you envy.

The next step is to assign one or more of the words from the inventory to a situation in your life, addressing either a resource, residence, or relationship. In the resources domain, which translates to money, job, material stuff, and so on, identify a person or people *with whom you have a relationship* and rate your envy of him or her based on this person's having something you desire. Now ask yourself how that envy has impacted the relationship domain with that person. When you go out to dinner, do you secretly wish he or she would pay because you think he or she has more resources than you? Now look at the residence domain. Do you wish you had the home of another or the stuff that goes into a home, like flat-screen televisions, a different car, a new kitchen?

Finally, look at relationships. Do you wish you had a more loving partner, a more understanding boss, or more thoughtful and compliant children? How are your envies and angers interfering with those goals? Take out the anger scale you made for the "Anger Versus Your PFC" exercise in Chapter Two. Begin assigning the idea of envy, the perception that someone has more than you, to that list. Now use your word list and assign a word and a degree of anger to your envy list. For example, is it irritating that your neighbor has a new car, or is it infuriating? Is it annoying that your boss prefers your

(continued)

coworker, or is it driving you "postal"? Once again, anything above a 5 places you at higher risk of acting out that anger in some form of aggression. You may see a pattern, often based on the fear that no matter how hard you try, you will not be able to achieve what someone else has. Being aware of such a pattern can help you avoid aggression: the dangerous result of untamed anger trying to get someone else to change. Check your envy list. Is it money, power, the place you live, the relationships you see enjoyed by others that you envy?

Self-doubt may be driving your envy. The reality is, there may be some things you will never be able to achieve, but most of what you need and desire is attainable. When I was younger, I wanted to be an Olympic wrestler. I know that will never happen, but I still take pleasure in watching college and Olympic wrestling, without the overlay of envy that would detract from the enjoyment of watching.

Your inventory of envy is a reality check. The envy you experience is usually based on low self-esteem and a worry that someone else may outdo you. As you learn about your anger due to envy, you will see how much of it gets in your way to success. Until you shift the locus of control from those limbic emotions to the planning ability of your PFC, you may be undermining your very ability to reach your goals. The inventory of envy allows you to step out of this limbic response into the PFC, where you can more realistically assess your strengths. As you learn to control your anger, you can take that power and begin influencing the world around you. You are already learning to do it now.

The first thing to do is to shift from malicious envy to benign envy. Malicious envy reinforces the belief that you will never be able to reach your goals. What small step can you take to shift that energy to motivation, the sine qua non of benign envy? For example, if you envy a peer's relationship with your boss, get to work a few minutes early and leave a few minutes late. During those extra minutes, check in with your boss and proactively seek additional work, do it well and in a timely way, and then seek some more. You want to reinvent the way you are seen by others, as a productive, reliable member of the team. This is a much better way of addressing your envy than maliciously sniping about your colleague at the watercooler.

If we all have evolved the same basic brain, others no doubt experience the envy you experience. Can you imagine that? Someone else may actually think you have more than he or she does. Thinking about it this way allows you to use that brain ability to compare sets of data, this time beginning to recognize what you do have and what another may not. Perhaps you don't have a mansion, but you have a home. Perhaps you have enormous debt, but you are not yet in jail. Perhaps you are unemployed, but you have time to look for a job or take a class to update your skills. How you approach your envy will have an impact on how you achieve the outcome, outsmart your anger, and turn it into motivation and success.

TRANSFORMING THE ENVY OF OTHERS

How do you respond to a person you think envies you? Some people become suspicious (see Chapter Four for more on suspicion and anger) and anxious, but others actually try to avoid malicious envy by being more generous. Several studies have found that people who recognized the potential for malicious envy toward them were more likely to be generous to those who had less. When you hear that Bill Gates, one of the richest men in the world, has given a generous donation to some charity, you may feel positive about him. But if you hear that Bill Gates is keeping all his resources to himself, you have a very different reaction.

From an evolutionary perspective, the generosity of someone with more resources does two things. It reduces some of their resources and increases the resource of others. This type of prosocial behavior has the potential to ward off danger, in that people who are in need or feeling envious might simply try to take something from the person who has more. But it also creates the promise of a future reciprocal behavior should the person with more ever need help. Indeed, charity and giving back are ways both to help someone who thinks you have more than he does and to give that person a chance to shift from malicious envy to benign envy.

Ultimately, envy is a powerful source of sadness and despair, the true danger of which is that it moves us further away from one another. Staying further away from one another, distancing and harboring anger, compels us to stay limbic, uncomfortable, and unfulfilled.

Eventually we begin to feel isolated. We create our own lonely in-group, fearful that an enormous out-group is waiting around the next banana tree to take our resources, residence, and relationships.

CHAPTER 4

Sense Suspicion

Suspicions that the mind, of itself, gathers, are but buzzes;
but suspicions that are artificially nourished and put into men's heads
by the tales and whisperings of others, have stings.

—Francis Bacon (1561–1626)

Brenda never really felt secure in her position at the law office as a junior attorney and always kept her eyes open for someone who might replace her. Mary, the young new lawyer the law partners hired, embodied Brenda's worry. Brenda watched with misgiving every time Mary would talk to the senior lawyers. As soon as a partner left the room, Brenda would look directly at Mary with a silent and challenging stare, convinced that Mary was trying to weasel her way into the firm's good graces. At every opportunity, Brenda would tell her coworkers that Mary was awfully nice, but wasn't a "good hire" because her work showed she didn't "have the chops" to work at the high level of the current team. Flattered by this type of comment, her colleagues started to suspect that Brenda was right. After all, Brenda had been with the company for three years and was well allied with her coworkers.

Brenda commented that in court Mary was too passive. Brenda began to step up her game, becoming more and more aggressive and forceful as she pummeled witnesses in the box. While the partners noticed Brenda winning more cases, at home her marriage started to suffer. Her husband noticed that Brenda was more irritable, and the two began to drift apart. As the tension rose at home, Brenda spent even more time at work and directed her anger and fury at Mary, continuing to undermine the naïve young lawyer. Mary began to make more and more mistakes and was unprepared in court, reinforcing Brenda's portrayal of her incompetence. So it came as no surprise to anyone that at her biannual review, Mary was let go. Brenda's efforts to sabotage a person she perceived as an aggressive competitor had worked. But on the day Mary was fired, Brenda came home to find a note from her husband that he was leaving and wanted a divorce. Brenda's anger and suspicion at work had spilled over into her home life, leaving a wake of destruction as if from an exploding bomb.

The psychological traps and maneuvers revealed in the story of Brenda and Mary are as typical today as when Sir Francis Bacon wrote his famous essay on suspicion four hundred years ago. Whether in national or office politics, in our own families or in casual relationships, suspicion continues to prove a poisonous germ that incites mistrust and leads us in only one direction—straight to anger.

It takes only a small kernel of suspicion to undermine a person's trust in another. Suspicion arises because we are afraid that someone is trying to take what we have. Although it can feel good for a while to have more resources, residence, or relationships, that good feeling becomes anxiety if we think our stuff is in danger. And that anxiety can turn to anger.

But when we learn to sense suspicion, we create the opportunity to gain control over this powerful impulse. In fact, you already have the tools to do this in your brain. You just need to learn how.

THE DARK SIDE OF SUSPICION

Suspicion is a form of anxiety, a perfectly normal emotion that evolved as a way to survive. Our ancestors who alerted to the rustling of a bush or the sound of a twig snapping were more likely to survive than those who did not pay attention: that sound could be the only warning of a predator stalking you for their lunch. But suspicion can also lead to far more sinister outcomes, induced by much more innocent events. Mary and Brenda's story is just one of a myriad of examples from our daily lives.

We don't know Mary's side of the story. We only know that she was younger and had a skill set similar to Brenda's. Given that Brenda was already deeply insecure about her job, Mary became a perfect, though totally *imaginary*, rival. Once Brenda allowed her suspicions that she could lose her job to Mary run unfiltered in her mind, she interpreted every signal from Mary as an affront and then created a rumor mill that led to Mary's dismissal. Her suspicion, of which she was only barely conscious, spread like a virus in Brenda's psyche. She only knew that she went to work feeling tense and fearful each day after Mary was hired.

Russell Haddelton, a colleague of mine who practices law, once wrote to me that "in depositions and on cross-examination, one technique which some lawyers use is to get the other guy so pissed off that he loses it. Once that happens, you have an enormous advantage. It is a lousy way to play the game, but some lawyers do it." Russ went on to tell me that anger in the courtroom even has a name: "Mongo." But all too often Mongo is not confined to the courtroom. As noted in the subtitle of an article in the *Legal Times*, "anger may help lawyers win in court, but not at home." Unfortunately, Brenda's suspicion and anger made her a casualty of the shrapnel from her own anger bomb.

This is the danger of suspicion. Most of the time, we don't even realize what we are actually feeling. With low levels of suspicion, we feel insecure, nervous, mildly threatened. But with high levels, our suspicion makes us feel defenseless, violated, and panicky. In extreme cases, this can lead to actual paranoia. Anxiety is a horrible feeling, a sense of impending, sometimes life-threatening doom. What better way to get rid of that sense of powerlessness than to become powerful? Rather than running away from danger, an avoidance behavior, the best thing your brain can devise is to attack, approach the threat, and drive it away. Suspicion can lead to remarkable and sometimes truly dangerous anger.

Think of it like this: suspicion is like dry timber waiting for a spark in our brains. At first we don't even notice it's there, but once aflame, it burns as fast and furious rage. In our day-to-day lives, suspicion can become an insidious force that undermines our ability to trust another human being, whether a coworker, a friend, or even a spouse. Looking at the big picture, suspicion is responsible for creating tiny tears in the social fabric that can, and regularly do, lead to the unraveling of relationships, the undoing of our residence, and our resources' hanging by a thread.

Exercise: How Suspicious Are You?

If I ask you whether you're someone who feels suspicion, you might say, "No way!" But think a little harder. Do you ever sense suspicion in these moments?

1. You see your colleague talking to your supervisor, and they both look over at you.

2. You see a car with two people in it looking at your house; they slow down as they drive by your yard.

3. You get an email from a company you recognize asking for your Social Security number.

4. You get a check at a restaurant charging for three desserts instead of the two you ordered.

5. You're standing in a loud, disorganized line to buy a deli sandwich when the person behind you seemingly tries to push ahead. You are really hungry and have been waiting longer.

6. Your partner is talking with an attractive stranger at a party.

7. Your child quickly turns off the computer when you come into the room.

8. You see a stranger on the opposite side of an empty street begin to cross over to your side.

9. Your car salesman tells you that you're getting the best deal possible.

10. You are watching a political debate between two candidates.

As you can see, suspicion is a completely normal sensation. And in question 5, you can see how suspicion very easily connects to and incites anger. I am just being honest when I say that I want that pushy guy in the deli line to get his "due." I want him to change what he is doing, and I want him to do it now. At that moment I am just another human being looking for food. And so is he. And as we all share basically the same brain, that person in the deli line may be feeling the same way I am about the other people in line, including me. Everyone at some time gets suspicious.

In all of the ten scenarios, at least one of the 3R's has been threatened. In the computer example, a parent may get suspicious that someone is trying to lure his or her child away, either through advertising, pornography, or a too robust social chat. A parent may also think that the child's turning off the computer so suddenly has taken away some parental control or compromised his or her role as a caregiver and provider. What was that kid doing or watching that he had to shut it down when you walked in the room? Parents know how angry this can make them, even as they still love and want to care for their kid. In one of the first stories in the book, about the teenage girl struggling with addiction, her parents were terrified and suspicious that the drugs were going to take their child away from them. And who knows what was going through Dan's mind as he struggled with his psychosis and perhaps paranoia?

At its root, suspicion is a primal emotion born out of the fear that someone will take what's yours (or should be yours), leaving you vulnerable and out in the cold. When we look at suspicion through the lens of our evolutionary three domains, it comes down to this: you fear someone might take your resources (food), your residence (shelter), or your relationships (mate). Brenda suspected that Mary would "take" her job, which impacted all three domains—food, shelter, and the relationships she had with her boss and coworkers. Mary may also have suspected that Brenda was out to get *her*, and *two* suspicious brains are a sure formula for disaster. Envy in one promotes suspicion in the other, and they feed off of each other in a vicious circle.

ENRAGED IN WAITING

Do you ever get annoyed when you're waiting in line and notice the line next to you going faster? Or when some guy tries to go directly to the head of the line you've been waiting in for a long time? Or when a new lane suddenly opens up, and the person behind you rushes ahead while you're still stuck in the old line? When you start to feel your blood pressure rising in these instances, it is a prime example of sensing suspicion. You're afraid that someone else is going to get a "resource" before you, and in our ancient struggle for survival, that just isn't fair, and places you at a potential disadvantage. People become unruly; they shout; they stomp out of stores, leaving their merchandise in the cart. Sometimes fights break out—all because of what researchers have called "queue rage."

For more than two decades, researchers from MIT's Center for Engineering Systems Fundamentals, led by Dr. Richard Larson, have been studying the psychology of people waiting in line. They found that people don't mind waiting, even for a long time, as long as the line is perceived as fair—first come, first served. Anger about this goes way back to our childhood: remember the feelings toward the kid who cut in line at school? We all recall the feeling of injustice when a teacher or lunch lady didn't do anything about it.

This is one reason we've begun to see checkout lines changing at large stores and banks, using the model we're familiar with at the airline check-in—the single line that feeds to the next available clerk. Think about it: Which kind of line would keep you a calmer and happier customer, one more likely to come again?

When we sense suspicion, it often starts out with anxiety caused by experiencing low-grade mistrust. How do you feel as you watch another car hover near the empty parking spot you have your eye on? And suspicion can sometimes be useful. Predators these days may not arrive on four legs baring fangs, but they still abound in designer suit jackets selling miracle cancer cures and running Ponzi schemes. How you react to the suspect situation is influenced by whether you go limbic and activate anger or use your PFC, recognize your anxiety, and just avoid getting involved with the suspect person or circumstance.

But most often in today's world, suspicion keeps people teetering on the edge of anger, in a constant state of unease. Unchecked, suspicion drives a wedge in potentially positive social interactions and, at the extreme, can lead to angry attacks against an imaginary foe. But we can begin to outsmart suspicion in our own minds—and the minds of others—by learning to understand where suspicion originates and why it remains with us.

THE SUSPICIOUS BRAIN

Feeling a basic level of mistrust is an automatic brain response to unfamiliar people. The survival mechanisms in the brain's limbic system that produce this feeling have evolved over millions of years and are not likely to go away anytime soon. Our brains, modern as we like to think they are, simply have not evolved to trust people instantly. Think about how your trust response is tested every day. Will you open your door to anyone who rings the buzzer? Do you think your mechanic is honest? Does the person asking you for a donation really represent that nonprofit group, or is it a scam?

Human beings have become very adept at looking at a face and deciding if the owner of that face can be trusted. Though trust may feel instantaneous, it is in fact *generated* through a complex process that links the feeling part of the brain to the thinking part. This was shown in one of the latest high-tech experiments conducted by Dr. Read Montague and his team from Baylor College of Medicine's Human Neuroimaging Laboratory. Study participants were asked to assess the motivation and intent of "anonymous" people, people they had never met, based on facial expressions. The team monitored simultaneous brain activity of pairs of strangers in different cities using a new technology they developed called "hyperscanning," in which researchers can synchronize live fMRI scanning of two inter-acting brains from different geographical locations.

Using a simple investment game in which the subjects had to decide how much money to give the other person, the researchers observed that trust was actually *formed* through a millisecond com-parative analysis in the cingulate cortex, a section of the limbic system involved in bonding and social interactions. From there, a signal was transmitted to the PFC, which analyzed the data and made a thinking assessment of whether or not that person could be trusted.

This assessment rapidly takes in a person's total presence—his or her face, eyes, body language—and quickly attributes intention and emotions to what we see. Based on our interpretation, we will respond with some combination of trust or mistrust, approach or avoidance. If we feel that we cannot trust a person, we avoid and move away. But if that person persists, we can also become angry and aggressive when we want the mistrusted person to back off. I've experienced my own suspicion sliding into anger with pushy salesman types and with those stubborn "squeegee men," the aggressive windshield cleaner guys standing around at highway intersections, who you suspect will spray your windshield without your consent and still expect a payment. What about in your experience?

But getting ripped off or being deceived was not the first thing that humans evolved to question. Our earliest concerns were based on a much more imperative need: to know quickly whether a person in our vicinity was safe. Groundbreaking research by Harvard University scientists in 2006 confirmed just how adept we are at determining this fundamental trust factor. In their study on first impressions, the researchers showed participants a series of both neutral and angry facial images. How long, they wondered, would it take a person to figure out the feeling behind that face? Seconds? Minutes? To their surprise, they had to measure the response in milliseconds, or thousandths of a second.

Our human brain decides whether a person can be trusted within a mere *39 milliseconds*, less than the amount of time it takes a world-class sprinter to spring from a starting block. The blink of an eye is between 300 and 400 milliseconds. There are 1,000 milliseconds in one second. And it only takes 39 milliseconds to figure out the meaning of a face. Not only that, we also have the ability to attribute the *degree* of risk: the angrier the face, these researchers found, the higher the possibility of threat. From a biological perspective, this makes a lot of sense—the ability to infer the intention of someone else holds enormous survival significance.

BRUSH UP YOUR TRUST RATING INSTANTLY

One of the simplest ways to improve other people's assessment of your trustworthiness is to appear as clean and polished as possible—this is what research by Sarah L. Moore and Kenneth Wilson from the Institute of Biological Sciences at the University of Stirling (Scotland) is indicating. Their studies with primates show that males who have fewer parasites make better mates; they attract both more female attention and more resources. The human translation? The more clean-cut you appear, the more likely you are to attract and generate trust in others. Think about the huge industry in hygiene products! Bottom line: brush your hair.

We mostly take this "instant" comparative analysis for granted—our brains just do this without conscious awareness or thinking about it. However, we are not born with this ability; it actually develops sometime during human infancy. Babies like faces. But not until around six months does a baby figure out that some faces are familiar and others are unfamiliar. A baby could not have the trust-distrust response unless able to distinguish between a familiar face and the face of a stranger. At this point in development, a baby may begin to cry when approached by an unknown face (person), something we commonly call stranger anxiety. Whether the face is angry or friendly is irrelevant; if the face is simply unfamiliar, most babies will cry. If you're a parent, you recognize this phenomenon and may have actually apologized to out-of-town family members who just want to hold your bundle of joy.

The evolution of our ability to make these distinctions early in life was probably protective. A defenseless baby unable to alert others with a loud cry when he or she saw an unfamiliar face could wind up as some animal's lunch. Try to remember that "suspicion" at this point in a baby's life might be a lifesaver, even though all you want to do is cuddle your wailing grandson.

FACE IT—YOUR FACE MATTERS

I'm reminded of this seemingly simple idea all the time. I went to the department store the other day to buy my wife a gift. There were two clerks at the perfume counter. They were equally "attractive" in terms of their external appearance, and both were alert and looking out for customers. But one seemed friendly, while the other seemed pushier, appearing more interested in making a sale than in helping customers get what they really needed or wanted. The friendly one was relaxed and smiling. She appeared welcoming and drew me in, and my limbic brain reacted with a sense of calm. This was a person who was not threatening to take my resources for her own gain. This was a sales-person who influenced my brain to trust her. She would help me find a product that my wife would like, enhancing the relationship and stability of my residence.

The other clerk elicited a different feeling: that she was pressuring me to buy something. I sensed that I was going to be exploited, that the expenditure of my economic resource was not going to enhance the relationship with my wife; I was in danger of being sold a product that would put my money in the salesperson's pocket, enhancing her resources at my expense. I did not trust her. Instead, I felt that she was trying to cheat me. What is remarkable is that these attributions of intent occurred in the blink of an eye. Only as I write about it now can I more thoroughly articulate the instantaneous thought process that occurred. But occur it did, and it does in all of us. Which clerk would you have picked to make your perfume purchase? Not the pushy one, right? She did not invite approach because instead of projecting trust, she conveyed that she was just after a commission. Her behavior and facial expression were emotional red lights. But how does that happen?

Driven by the need to understand the brain's role in human interaction, scientists at many universities worldwide are studying how our faces affect our brains—not just how facial expressions make us feel emotionally, but what happens inside the brain geography when we look at other human faces. Most experts agree that even just looking at *pictures* of emotional facial expressions activates certain brain structures. In numerous neuroimaging studies, a smile has been shown to light up the PFC—your "thinking" brain area. But a scowl lights up the limbic area—your "feeling" brain area. All of us can and should use this information to our advantage. If we want to make a sale or even a friend, it behooves us to don our most trusting and friendly facial expressions, appealing to another person's rational PFC instead of triggering a limbic reaction. Just like in the musical *Annie*, "You're never fully dressed without a smile."

The next time you're in a restaurant, take a look at the faces of the people around you. It's pretty easy to gauge the emotional gist of their conversations based on their facial expressions. Some are laughing and animated; others might be serious or dour—this is because people in conversation stimulate each other's brains. But look at someone dining alone—it's nearly impossible to tell what he or she is thinking.

In fact, people rarely think about the facial expression they're wearing. We think about our clothes, our hair, and our shoes—details people don't always notice. But what is noticed first—our facial expression—is hardly given a second thought. If we are trying to help others put their trust in us and let down their guard, we need to remember that our facial expressions have a lot of power to do that. The more open and friendly we appear, the more likely it is that we are willing to engage. If people can't read our expression, they will become more easily suspicious of us. People will always have a response to faces—the level of trust you want to project to others is entirely up to you. What are you wearing on your face right now?

It's interesting to note how rarely the human face is static; it's a complex and ever-changing panorama. When it comes to determining whom we can trust, we are dealing with a moving target. Our faces are the external expression of internal and invisible parts of our personality and character. And when a feeling state or a thinking state changes inside, very often it is reflected by a change in our face. I was reminded of this recently when watching the faces of fellow Red Sox fans at Fenway Park when the Yankees were in town. A pinstripe batter was up with the bases loaded and two outs. When the bat struck, sending a fly ball to right field, every face shifted to agony as the right fielder went back, back, back. When he was up against the bullpen, the ball flew harmlessly into his glove. All those faces, first tense and worried, transformed into portraits of excitement and relief. Fear and suspense shifted instantaneously into contentment and joy. This situation, of course, was easy to analyze. But often, changing expressions can send challenging mixed messages.

So how do we process these changing tides of emotion to generate trust and move away from suspicion? To address this question, a team of researchers from the University of Wurzburg explored how our brain responds when we see a face changing expressions, shifting from one emotion to another. In their 2010 study published in *Social Cognitive and Affective Neuroscience*, they showed video clips of the onset and offset of happy and angry facial expressions to a group of subjects while the subjects were hooked up to an fMRI brain imager. When a happy face became an angry face, the researchers saw activity move from the observer's amygdalae, two almond-shaped masses located deep within the temporal lobes in the limbic region, to the PFC. *Almost as if in dialogue,* these two parts of the brain—the ancient and the new—were deep in consultation. The amygdalae recognized a shift in the mood and, therefore, the potential threat in the face. They sent an instant message to the PFC, which then assessed the change in the internal thoughts and feelings expressed by the face and decided what to do. This internal brain dialogue was demonstrated both for static faces, in Montague's research, as well as for the changing faces in the Wurzburg research. Our brain is designed to communicate with itself.

The assessments you make of another person happen so quickly that you may not even be aware of why you begin to feel differently than you did a millisecond before. Your feeling of suspicion does not arise in a vacuum; your brain has detected what it thinks may be a shift in the danger equation of the surroundings. At first it is only a feeling, an emotional perception. It is then up to your PFC to process the information, decipher and interpret if there really is a threat, and then decide on an action. If the limbic response is too overwhelming, it can interfere with the decision-making and evaluative process of the PFC, even to the point of communicating misinformation on which the PFC has to base its action plan. This is where unharnessed suspicion can lead to a very poor and unproductive outcome. Remember the Brenda and Mary drama at the beginning of the chapter?

THE EYES HAVE IT

What is the first part of the face you naturally look at to know what someone is thinking or feeling? Just as with facial expressions, eye

THE EYE CONTACT EFFECT

With so many people distracted by phone devices lately, it's becoming nearly impossible to have a conversation without at least one person averting his or her gaze and attention else-where. Although people don't mean to be rude, their lack of attention and eye gaze is disrupting to what we call a "social brain network." When they do this, they are sending someone else's brain a message of disrespect, disinterest, and at times frank disregard. Any one of these would make you angry, and as we all share the same basic brain, your distraction probably makes someone else angry as well.

Studies show that averting your gaze can be a form of "silent treatment," effectively saying that the other is not worth looking at, that he or she has no value. In essence, it is a fairly clear form of disrespect and a major trigger for anger. So when we don't look at someone we're talking to, we are saying, "This text message is more important than you are." How many times have we been annoyed with our kid or someone else who is texting or answering a cell phone while sitting at dinner with us? Why do we get angry and suspicious? Because without the sense that we are valued, we worry that we are dispensable, which means we are vulnerable to being attacked in a jungle of limited resources. Remember, the limbic brain that feels this is hundreds of millions of years old. It is our PFC—our new brain—that has the tools to overcome this deep-seated suspicion.

Keep this in mind the next time your cell phone buzzes while you are with someone. When you avert your gaze, you increase the chances of losing respect and trust because you are essentially not communicating those attributes to your associate, friend, or loved one.

contact can help build trust, binding another person to you and you to him or her in a mutual feeling of safety, the antithesis of suspicion. But the opposite can also be true; improper or misinterpreted eye contact can start a war.

Eye contact is currently a thriving area of scientific research because it provides clues about how humans interpret the intentions, thoughts, and feelings of other people. In a 2009 study led by Dr. Atsushi Senju at the University of London's Centre for Brain and Cognitive Development, researchers discovered that the ancient parts of our brain, not the more recently evolved neocortex, are the first to activate when eye contact is made or even averted. As expected, the signal from the limbic region is then sent to the PFC, which quickly processes the information. Our brain compares the incoming data with memory of past experience and facial expressions, our personal trust-mistrust scale, and approach and avoidance patterns so fast that everything seems to happen all at once.

We all know from personal experience that eye contact elicits various thoughts and feelings. Is this a gaze of challenge, of sexual interest, of admonishment? Such interpretations may feel automatic and instantaneous, but they weren't always. At some point in our personal development, we had to figure out if Mom was angry or proud, if our buddy was serious or joking, if our girlfriend or boy-friend was inviting or discouraging.

This interpretation of eye gaze information starts very young and has been of interest to researchers in developmental psychology worldwide. Ongoing research by a team of scientists at Tilburg University in the Netherlands has explored the development of gaze and visual attention in babies. One study suggested that the infant's brain is rapidly forming connections and new pathways linking the ancient limbic system to the modern PFC by laying down a circuitry of brain "roads." This complicated but elegant infrastructure results in a brain network dedicated to interpreting social interactions.

This is an incredibly exciting discovery, as it allows us to finally pinpoint the key brain region through which we learn to be social beings and can begin to control the storm of our emotions. When a baby can finally distinguish between self and other, he or she can experience all the emotions that stem from social relationships; feelings like love, anger, envy, suspicion, pride, shame, and joy slowly develop. Each of us was once a baby. Each of us at some point entered the world of social interaction, rife with the potential to trust and mistrust. As children we reacted on impulse, but as adults we can exercise and develop our ability to let our "new" brain do the thinking. Armed with the knowledge of how our brain structures affect our behaviors, we can overcome the suspicion that our resources, residence, and relationships are in jeopardy by shifting out of the limbic jungle and into the enlightenment of our PFC.

TOO CLOSE FOR COMFORT

In addition to reacting to the facial data and eye contact we have evolved to process, our suspicion radar is also triggered by the simple geography of body placement. If someone stands too close to us, we are instantly suspicious of nefarious intent. We've all had that experience. When someone violates the unwritten rule about the appropriate (but unmeasured) perimeter of no-entry around our body—our "personal space"—we begin to feel uncomfortable. When we accidentally touch someone, we instantly apologize, and expect the same if we are touched without consent. Even though we know that nine times out of ten, such "space invasion" is probably innocent and unintentional, we instantly become suspicious of a person who is simply too close to our body.

Being aware of this unspoken distance has served me well in my practice. There are times when getting too close will only increase the anguish and paranoia of a patient. But keeping a safe and respectful distance allows the patient to engage with me from his or her own bubble of security. One of my patients, an eight-year-old girl, suffered intense anxiety when she had to speak with anyone she did not know well, and could not tolerate being face-to-face in my office. We over-came that difficulty by sitting on opposite sides of the room, our backs to each other, and using plastic toy phones to talk. Using this tech-nique, the girl was able to engage in a way in which she felt safe and respected, eventually turning around and facing me, but still using the phone to communicate with me.

Where does this sense of personal space come from? And why does its violation make us nervously suspicious? You should know the answer by now: it comes from our limbic brain, specifically the amyg-dalae. Research on the amygdalae has shed new light on how these tiny brain regions serve to protect our personal safety boundaries. A fascinating 2009 study by a group of scientists from the California Institute of Technology (CIT) published in the journal *Nature Neuro-science* examined what happens when the amygdalae are not present. The study focused on a remarkable but unfortunate woman who had the most complete loss of amygdalae function known to scien-tists. The woman, who lost both her amygdalae due to an extremely rare genetic disorder that causes Urbach-Wiethe disease, could not detect any boundaries of interpersonal space. She understood the *concept* of interpersonal space, even remarking that she did not want to make the examiner uncomfortable by standing too close. But despite this cognitive awareness, her spatial awareness was nil; as one of the study's researchers noted, "On one trial she walked all the way toward the experimenter to the point of touching, and she repeatedly stated that any distance felt comfortable."

The amygdalae are important in mediating face-to-face and body-to-body interactions by modulating the response of the PFC. According to the CIT researchers, when study participants perceived someone as coming too close, their amygdalae (those that were healthy and intact) showed strong activity. So from an evolutionary survival point of view, the amygdalae are saying, "Hey, PFC. Be sure that this person keeps a certain distance, just in case their intentions are not pure." Indeed, this ancient and primitive part of our emotional

THE AUTHORITY OF
THE AMYGDALAE

What happens when one of our brain regions is impaired? How can the PFC make a cogent and rational decision if the data it obtains from the limbic system are skewed, distorted, or simply absent? One of the most fascinating areas of brain study, particularly as it relates to the dialogue between the amygdalae and the PFC, has to do with Williams syndrome (WS), a genetically induced condition in which a particular portion of one's DNA is absent. Approximately one in ten thousand individuals worldwide is born with this neurodevelopmental disorder first identified by New Zealander Dr. J.C.P. Williams in 1961.

This genetic deletion results in some remarkable behaviors: most people with WS have some mild to severe learning disabilities and cognitive challenges, though some have strong verbal skills and great memories, and have distinctive "elfin" physical characteristics. But the most amazing and consistent trait, now firmly ascribed to the genetic deletion, is their friendly and outgoing personality. I recently met a nine-year-old with WS who was one of the friendliest and gentlest people I have ever met. In fact, this unique friendliness on the part of folks with WS is teaching us a lot about the role of the amygdalae in our development of suspicion and trust.

Individuals with WS have a complete lack of suspicion. For as yet unknown reasons, this unique genetic deletion results in strikingly high sociability and empathy toward others. People with WS are universally welcoming and trusting. In a thought-provoking study published in 2009, scientists at Stanford University's Center of Interdisciplinary Brain Science found that the amygdalae of WS subjects became active when seeing happy faces, but that activity in the brain region practically stopped when shown fearful faces. Fear expressed on the face simply did not register in the WS subjects' brains. Another recent study from France revealed that WS children also have a difficult time identifying angry faces. If you can't detect anger, it is very difficult to be suspicious.

These critical studies provide key evidence of the crucial function of the amygdalae in the formation of social emotion as well as how the PFC processes those emotions. WS has also been studied by the National Institute of Mental Health. This research finally establishes the "wireless" connection between the ancient and modern parts of our brains and how we are able to modulate our anger or any other emotion.

center gets a starring role in how we perceive potential danger, a pathway of suspicion. The amygdalae provide information that is communicated to the PFC. The PFC can then take our perceptions and make rational assessments and decisions in response.

It's worth noting here that the degree of acceptable body proximity varies from culture to culture. If you've ever traveled to China, you may have noticed a difference in the perception of personal space—it's much closer than in the United States, or even neighboring Japan, and at first it can feel uncomfortable. But you, and your amygdalae, will adjust very quickly to what's appropriate for your safety. However, in every culture, too close is just too close.

Not only is proximity a factor, but a 2011 study out of the University of Essex in the United Kingdom revealed that we are primed to detect angry body posture as well as angry faces. This also makes evolutionary sense, as sometimes faces are hidden by masks or shadows. Being able to detect a body displaying a threat gesture gives us a survival edge and perhaps even a chance to get away.

SUSPICIOUS MINDS

The vast majority of human beings are intrinsically interested in what other people think or feel. We call that empathy. But we are particularly interested in what other people are thinking about *us*. This can be rewarding if we are secure in our own self-image, but nerve-racking if we are not. For many people, the reason they feel suspicion of others has a lot to do with how they feel about themselves, particularly when they're feeling insecure. For instance, I once had a patient who was extremely worried that other people saw him as insecure. He started asking other people if they thought he was insecure. His asking made them think he was insecure, leading my patient to feel more insecure. Strikingly, he even worried in our sessions whether he was a good enough patient.

This perpetual cycle of insecurity is not unique to my patient. Studies have shown that it can develop into a consistent phenomenon impacting the perception of other people in that person's life. Investigators at the University of New Hampshire, led by Dr. Edward Lemay, demonstrated in a 2009 study that people who tend to worry that others see them as insecure are in fact more likely to actually

THE FACEBOOK SUSPICION CHALLENGE

If you happen to be in a new relationship with someone, do not go on Facebook. The more you use Facebook, it turns out, the more likely you are to become suspicious and jealous of your romantic partner. This was the conclusion reached by research psychologists from the University of Guelph, Ontario, in a 2009 study that surveyed several hundred university students who regularly used Facebook.

The Facebook-induced jealousy was attributed to the ambiguous information the students would receive about their partner—information they wouldn't otherwise have access to. Of note, 75 percent of those surveyed said they had previous romantic or sexual partners as "friends" on Facebook, and close to 80 percent reported that their partner also had previous partners as "friends." Knowing this, people could "learn" about their ex's past, and Facebook enabled increased exposure to imaginary "deceptions." The researchers also noted that the Facebook visits became addictive, further distorting the PFC's ability to think clearly as it became overwhelmed with suspicion.

"It fosters a vicious cycle," one researcher said. "If one partner in a relationship discloses personal information, it increases the likelihood that the other person will do the same, which increases the likelihood of jealousy."

Have you ever felt suspicious on Facebook? This might start off in the form of general "curiosity." For instance, "Hmm, who is that girl? Let me just click to learn more." Maybe you found something that looked like a "clue" to some relationship you didn't know about or were excluded from. Now your suspicion wolfhounds are out. Can you talk yourself out of this fictional "affair" now? Try it. What is reality: your relationship or a vague, nonexistent association on a computer social network?

Facebook is not going away anytime soon, but as we can with all sources of suspicion, we can take it to the PFC, which will tell us, "Your suspicions are in your limbic system, so don't get all bent out of shape. Don't go limbic. Keep it frontal." So try staying off Facebook if you are just starting to date someone or if you already know you're the jealous type. Life is too short to be letting your mind invent drama where there really is none.

be insecure. Here's the reason this happens: if I think you see me as insecure, my limbic system reads this as disrespect, as my not being valued. As a result, I get anxious and begin the slide toward anger. As it turns out, people with the lowest self-esteem often have the shortest fuse. They perceive everything people say about them as a criticism, which in turn fuels their insecurity and keeps their limbic systems on constant alert. The study also noted that there could be a resistance to hearing negative feedback from a partner, even if it is intended as helpful. This resistance can lead to resentment and mistrust in the insecure partner, and a sense by the more secure partner of having to compromise what he or she says. In this way, both partners can wind up feeling powerless, leading to two limbic brains and to more anger.

You have probably known individuals like this, and I have seen this frequently among my patient population. One recent case is a good example. In family therapy, nobody could say anything to "Maggie" without her flying off the handle, getting nasty, and being verbally aggressive. Her brother and parents would clarify that they were not being critical, and she would calm and settle for a period of time. But a small remark or a sudden change of expression caught out of the corner of her eye would spark the tinder and she would be off again with no clear provocation. Her fragile belief in herself would crack, brittle as the crust of a crème brûlée.

When she regrouped, the family would then continue the session, hopeful that the anger had passed. What she had seen in the faces of her family, I had not. To me it appeared that they treated her with respect, easily forgiving and willing to overlook her transgressions. I wondered how much she really trusted them and how her suspicions led her to constantly question their intentions.

With time and a willingness to tolerate these difficult emotions, Maggie and her family began to recognize how sensitive she was to their perceived critiques. She learned to reinterpret a facial expression or a body movement from one of threat to one of peace, and was able to change the way she presented herself. She was retraining the information provided to her PFC by her amygdalae. This movement toward peace allowed them all to be more empathic with one another, and this interest and concern served as a platform for clear communication. At the end of each session, I would thank them for sitting with me, and eventually they began to thank one another for the shared desire and goal to be a family based on trust rather than suspicion.

OPENING MINDS: OUR INFLUENCE ON OTHERS

By now it should be clear that we have all evolved the same basic brain architecture. We are all wired in about the same way when it comes

PARANOIA—THE ULTIMATE IN SUSPICION

In my clinical practice, I frequently engage with patients who are not only suspicious but frankly paranoid. They may see conspiracies and plots everywhere. A simple gesture can be misperceived as a lethal threat. One of my favorite stories has to do with when I was doing my oral examinations for the psychiatry boards. Candidates interviewed a patient in front of three examiners. On occasion the proctor overseeing the examination would also come into the room. And that particular year, the Board of Psychiatry and Neurology itself was being examined by a regulatory group charged with approving or disapproving its accreditation. Candidates could have up to six or seven people observing their oral examination of a patient.

The examination took place in a small office. I sat waiting for my volunteer patient, a man recruited from the psychiatric inpatient unit of the hospital where the exam was taking place. Behind me sat the three examiners. The unit psychiatrist

(continued)

brought in the man I was going to interview. He sat across from me, facing the door and the three people behind me. As he began telling me his story, his paranoia was almost palpable. He was convinced he had been poisoned during a boxing match that had happened the year before, that the poison was still in his body, and that it placed him in contact with aliens, alerting them to his every position.

As he told me the story, the examiner of the examiners entered the room. I could see my volunteer's body tense. We went on. But then, three more observers entered the room. Now my volunteer was ready to jump out of his skin. He stopped talking, and, alerted to the perceived danger, his body tensed, his brow began to furrow, and I could tell he was about ready to try to fight or flee. He asked what all these people were doing in the room, perhaps suspecting that they were all aliens who had found out where he was.

Even as his body became tense, I purposely became more relaxed. Making eye contact with him, I asked him to pause for a second, and turned to face the people behind me. Asking them also to wait, I turned back to my volunteer. With my hands raised around the level of my waist, fingers spread, palms visible, my gesture tried to communicate the idea of slowing things down. I assured him that he was not the one being examined here, but that I was. If he wanted to stop, we could absolutely do so, but all those people behind me were there to see what I was doing, not what he was doing. Because his anxiety was acknowledged and his fear allayed, he began to calm, and we went on with the interview. By treating him with respect and reminding him of his control and influence over the interview process, I was able to decrease his suspicion and defuse his brewing anger. As an aside, I am convinced that had I done anything else, he would have stormed out of the room, and I probably would have failed my exam!

to responding to certain signals with either trust or suspicion. Knowing this allows us to send appropriate signals to others because we are also the subject of suspicion ourselves.

Ever notice how you can tell when someone has had a change of heart? Sometimes your "instincts" tell you that it is probably a better "idea" to keep away from a person. A change in another's demeanor activates a change in your choice of whether to approach or avoid. But if someone else can activate your decisions, changes in *your* demeanor will also impact the approach or avoidance of someone else. This insight is critical because it means that you have influence over other people. Now you just have to decide what kind of influence you want to have. If you project suspicion, you are likely to make other people suspicious as well, leading them to avoid you.

Have you ever thought that someone felt suspicious of you and didn't trust you? Most of us have, and it doesn't feel good. The other person might look away or tilt his head to the side as opposed to facing you directly. If you notice that someone appears less likely to engage, is trying to move away, averts eye contact, or subtly adjusts her body in a defensive posture, it may mean that you have, even unwittingly, created an impression of threat. You have activated a limbic system response in this person. With what you know about your own facial expressions, eye gaze, and body contact, you now have the tools to change others' suspicion, defusing the potential for anger. You defuse another person's limbic reaction toward you by appearing to be relaxed, open, and friendly. For instance, when I encounter a haphazard line in the drug store, I always ask those already waiting where the end of the line is. They all immediately relax because I have respected their place in line. This also opens the door to a conversation while we wait, which allays everyone's suspicions.

I am always amazed at how much suspicion can be alleviated by doing simple things like opening a door and letting someone else go first. We have all experienced having two people get to a door at the same time, perhaps at the supermarket. When one of the people goes in front of the other, that person is frequently suspected of being selfish, creating an impression that she thinks the world revolves around her. Mistrust and suspicion are activated in the brain of the person who has to go second. But when that first person instead holds the door open and says, "After you," to the second, an entirely different brain phenomenon occurs. I see this all the time, and also enjoy the astonishment of the other person. In some ways it is sad that he is astonished at all, anticipating that I would be just another selfish, oblivious person determined to go first.

TAKING CHARGE OF SUSPICION: USING YOUR PFC

Having amygdalae wired for instant and absolute trust of other human beings may sound charming to a degree. But for people with Williams syndrome, this can also be a liability, because they have limited ability to learn and adopt strategies to better interpret the signals sent by other people. The good news for most people is that these interpretive skills can be easily strengthened by practicing shifting awareness from our limbic system to the PFC. Let's see how this works from your own perspective. The following exercise will heighten your awareness of the work done by the PFC. Like any "muscle," the more you use it, the better it can work for you when you need it.

Exercise: Sorting Suspicion

Suspicion, like anger and envy, can appear in many forms and in varying degree. Arrange the following set of words into your personal "suspicion scale," rating them from 1 to 10: *suspicion, wariness, skepticism, doubt, misgiving, distrust, disbelief, paranoia, fear, alarm, dread, panic, trepidation, apprehension, concern, foreboding, unease.*

Read through your list of anger triggers from Chapter Two, Recognizing Rage, and place a check mark next to those that you now know stem from suspicion. For example, you may have been angry at your boss for being disrespectful, but now you realize that this was really a fear that your boss would try to ruin your career if you ever decided to look for another job. Place a *T* by the items on your list that you feel are valuable but on which you have a tenuous hold. Place an *I* by the items you see as your inadequacies or areas of incompetence. Place a *V* by the items that are vulnerable. Are you suspicious of anyone who seems to be better than you are in those areas? Place an *S* by those items, and the initials of that person or people. Write one of the words that describe the degree of suspicion. For example, two of the items on my list of anger triggers would now look like this:

✓ Disrespectful boss (7, anger), I (Inadequate, trepidation)
✓ Scratch on your car (6, displeasure), V (Vulnerable, wariness)

Once armed with your list of suspicion sources, you can sort suspicion into the three domains: resources, residence, and relationships. Organize your list by placing your items in one of those three domains. For instance, let's look at relationships. This is where being honest with yourself gets hard. In your family, do you suspect that your sister gets nicer presents for her birthday? That your children are using drugs? That your partner is cheating on you? In the first case, the fear is that your parents' love will be taken from you, in the second that your image as a good and aware parent will be taken from you, and in the third that your partner will be taken from you. Assign each person a place on your suspicion scale. Do this same exercise for resources and residence. My two example items now look like this:

Relationship: ✓ Disrespectful boss (7, anger), I (Inadequate, trepidation)
Resource: ✓ Scratch on your car (6, displeasure),V (Vulnerable, wariness)

You have now begun training your brain to use the PFC as a tool to recognize and then evaluate the sources of your anger, with its subsets of envy and suspicion. By being honest about your suspicions, you move them from a limbic response to a PFC assessment. Why?

Because honesty, morality, and the ability to forgive live in the PFC. Suspicion is part of our dark and shadowy maze of emotions and, as such, can distort our impression of events, leading us to suspect menace where none may exist. But menace can only be inferred if we don't encourage or allow our brain to compare it to "not-menace." But as we all have evolved basically the same brain, when we learn how to sense our own suspicions, we are also learning how to sense other people's suspicions of us.

Comparing sets of information in order to make the best decision is something our brains have been learning to do since our infant days of "stranger anxiety." This is a fundamental, continual, and fluid process of the human brain. In fact, this proclivity of our brain to compare pieces of information provides an inroad to generating a response in another person's brain: we can influence how someone else views us in those first thirty-nine milliseconds. In the next chapter, we will learn that even that tiny bit of time is enough to outsmart and defuse his or her potential anger.

CHAPTER 5

Project Peace

If you wish to experience peace, provide peace for another.
—Tenzin Gyatso, the fourteenth Dalai Lama (1935–)

Let us ever remember that our interest is in concord, not in conflict; and that our real eminence rests in the victories of peace, not those of war.
—William McKinley (1843–1901)

I came home one day to find a stranger putting up a yard sale sign on my front lawn. At first I was fairly annoyed. What business did this guy have putting a sign on my lawn? I got out of my car and approached him, at which point he bristled, and I sensed a defiant attitude. I felt my limbic response kicking in, but then consciously shifted to my PFC. In a calm and gentle tone, I asked what he was doing. His response was defensive: he was putting his sign next to the fire hydrant by the front lawn, and because it was public property, he had a right to do so. Rather than confront him, I joked that I really didn't mind if he was putting up a sign, just as long as he wasn't endorsing any political candidate I may oppose. He calmed, I calmed, and we began to engage in a rather remarkable conversation.

He was having a yard sale to clean out his basement, which was full of his late wife's belongings. It had taken him three years to do so, and was an important acknowledgment of her death. He told me that one morning, waiting for her to come down for breakfast, he decided to bring her coffee in bed. He entered the room to find her peaceful, without an expression of pain or worry on her face, but unresponsive and not breathing. His eyes welled with tears as he spoke, this man who just a few moments before had been a burly stranger engaged in a meaningless defensive posture.

This story demonstrates the extraordinary power of projecting peace. Had I continued my approach in anger, I would never have had the opportunity to establish a bond of trust between us or gain a glimpse into my neighbor's world.

THE POWER OF PEACE

You've spent the first four chapters of this book learning how to recognize your own limbic responses to life within the context of protecting or seeking the 3R's: resources, residence, and relationships. But as I noted in an earlier chapter, very often it is not your anger that gets in the way of your success. Instead, it is the anger of *others* that gets in the way—*their* envy or *their* suspicion. Anger is an emotion designed to change the behavior of someone else, so when someone is angry at you, he or she wants you to change. And that could impact the choices you need to make to achieve success. Another person's anger can have a huge effect on you.

But what if you could modulate another person's anger so that both of you can be more successful? You can. The first three steps in this book—Recognize Rage, Envision Envy, and Sense Suspicion—are about identifying your own anger. The next four steps will show you how to redirect the anger of those around you. With practice, you can become a master of each of these next four steps, starting with Project Peace.

Although we all have different triggers for our anger, our limbic responses are actually quite similar. We throw up our guard or we lash out. But when we step back and "keep it frontal" by using our PFC, rather than losing our cool—"going limbic"—we are able to disarm the anger response from others, just as I was able to do with my neighbor in the chapter-opening story. We can bring another person's limbic reaction under control by sending a clear message that we are no threat to him or her.

Starting with the first step, I recognize rage and that you are angry about something. But I am a fellow human being who understands the anger response and the fact that it is entirely normal—no different from hunger, thirst, or pain. Knowing that anger is a normal part of being human, I do not activate my own limbic fight-or-flight response, which would activate yours. When I do not get angry, I decrease the chance that you will get angry. When you see that I do not think I have more power than you, you don't need to be envious. When you see that I am not envious that you have more than I do, you don't need to be suspicious that I am trying to take your resources, residence, or relationship. All of this begins to happen when I send a message to you that I am not a threat and that you do not need to try and change my behavior. Projecting peace is the first step in defusing anger in others so that progress can be made for all.

On its face, projecting peace might seem simple—act peaceful to calm people down, right? We all can do this sometimes without much effort. The greater challenge lies in being able to do this when you least expect you might have to, and to do it consistently. In the beginning, projecting peace can prove to be a great behavioral challenge. There are three main reasons that account for this difficulty. First, there's the matter of biology. When someone displays anger toward us, our own limbic response—designed and refined over millennia for self-preservation—is instant and defensive. We immediately activate our fight-flight-freeze mode and usually display anger as an immediate response to the anger we perceive. Just as that person has engaged anger to get us to change our behavior, we respond with anger to get him or her to stop being angry. This rarely works. Instead, a vicious cycle ensues—a nonstop Ping-Pong of limbic assaults. This pattern is the same whether it's two children fighting over a toy, an unhappily married couple bickering, gang retaliation hits, or international wars. The pattern does not stop until the cycle is broken by rational action that comes from the frontal lobes of the brain—the PFC.

Second, we are not well instructed in how to learn and practice PFC control. In general, children everywhere are taught to restrain innate behaviors that are seen as negative: not to hit, not to be selfish, not to be rude. We try to teach our children to play nicely, share with others, and be polite and kind. But as a population we are not well educated about, nor do we routinely think about, how our biological impulses direct our actions and often mislead us.

Many of us do indeed figure these things out over time, and those who do have a responsibility to share that knowledge with those who do not, in a peaceful way that is not threatening or condescending. It just makes common sense to want a world that is less angry. We have seen the result of not including everyone in this learning process, and it is costly: an angrier society; a more aggressive society; a society convinced that resources, residence, and relationships are limited; and, as a result, a more violent society.

We continue to see examples of this every day, popularized by shows like *Jerry Springer*, where guests are goaded and provoked into displays of rage, cheered on by a salivating audience seeking vicarious thrills. Video games bring wars and conflicts into our living room, and social gaming connects groups of strangers pitted in battle against groups of others. The anonymity of social media and chat rooms has led to a new phenomenon, cyber-bullying, whereby a target can no longer escape even in the sanctuary of his or her own home.

With education, though, human behaviors can change. It wasn't too long ago that anger-fueled and antisocial behaviors like domestic abuse and drunken driving were ignored, if not tolerated, but that is beginning to change, at least in most societies. Domestic violence is no longer tolerated, parents are held accountable if their kids have parties with underage drinkers, and athlete-heroes are given hefty sanctions if they demonstrate violence and poor sportsmanship in front of adoring fans. Better judgment can help us make smarter decisions and reduce anger, violence, and crime. Building on this progress will involve learning how to exercise our PFC to rein in those limbic lunges. Should it be so far-fetched to teach age-appropriate neurobiology in elementary school, rather than waiting to send offenders to anger management classes in prison, after they've committed a crime?

Third, we are simply not wired to trust others instantaneously. As you have read in the earlier chapters and no doubt experienced in your daily life, strong and impulsive feelings like envy and suspicion have been embedded in the human brain system for millions of years. Such protective and adaptive feelings do not disappear overnight (nor should they completely). We are constantly in the process of making choices about whom to trust and who will be a threat, and these judgments are made in mere milliseconds. We base these judgments on what we perceive. Is the person attractive? Does she seem likeable, trustworthy, competent? Does he look like someone who can become aggressive? Researchers at Princeton University studied reaction times to first impressions of unfamiliar faces. They flashed a picture of a face for just one hundred milliseconds, way less than the blink of an eye. Within that brief time the subjects decided who was trustworthy and who was not. We now know that by thirty-nine milliseconds, the decision was made. And the longer the research participants studied a potentially untrustworthy face, the more negative and mistrustful they became.

What the Princeton study tells us is that we have a very narrow window in which to induce and garner trust from others: within one hundred milliseconds, your face can convey to another brain that you are peaceful. Projecting peace within the blink of an eye is absolutely essential to successfully laying a foundation for future trust. This may sound impossible, but in fact, you are exquisitely designed to do it.

MIRROR NEURONS CAN PROJECT PEACE

It might seem unfair to be given such a miniscule amount of time to make an impression. But the good news is that human beings are inherently capable of projecting peace when they approach others thoughtfully, leading with the PFC. Your very demeanor has a direct psychological—and even biological—influence on another person. Recent neuroscientific discoveries have shown that our brain wiring has evolved superbly to copy another person's actions and behaviors.

The first time this phenomenon was observed was in 1996, when a team of researchers from the University di Parma in Italy recorded the brain waves from 532 neurons in two macaque monkeys. When one monkey watched another monkey grasp a peanut, brain cells in the observing monkey fired as if it were performing the same action. These neurons were located in the premotor cortex, the part of the brain responsible for preparing the body for action: it is a brain region involved with intention, with anticipating a future movement. In essence, the brains of the observing monkeys were "mirroring" the monkeys they were watching. These brain cells were aptly named mirror neurons. Subsequent studies over the last few years have shown that humans also share a mirror neuron system, but one that is smarter, more specialized, and even more evolved than the monkey neurons. "We are exquisitely social creatures," said Dr. Cattaneo Rizzolatti, among the authors of the groundbreaking Italian study. "Our survival depends on understanding the actions, intentions and emotions of others." What is remarkable is that your brain has an influence on these perceptions of intention, which in turn have so much impact on thoughts and then feelings; each of us has an influence over the perceptions of all the other brains with which we come in contact.

Millions of years ago, an individual's survival would have depended on the rapid reading of social cues, especially facial expression or physical display. It would have behooved our very early ancestors to be able to read the expression of fear on the faces of their companions. Danger could be near, and it would be a good survival strategy for others to get scared as well so that all could take protective action. If your neighbor were angry at someone else, it could mean that you were also being threatened by that person and should be angry as well, especially if the protection of resources, residence, and relationships was involved. This makes clear evolutionary sense.

The discovery of mirror neurons has shown us a fascinating internal picture of how our brains adapted to enable survival. It has established a completely new understanding of social interaction and learning. Mirror neurons have important implications for how one person has the ability to influence another by eliciting his or her evolutionary predisposition to imitate the actions, thoughts, and perhaps feelings of another human being.

Studies suggest that mirror neurons serve more than just a muscular mimicry of a face. This is not just reaching for a banana because you see someone else doing it. Our brain's mirror mechanism also has an emotional component, a promising evolutionary process on which we may be able to piggyback as we try to calm the limbic brain of another person. When we see someone cry, our mirror neurons start analyzing how to replicate the muscles of facial expression, retrieving a compatible emotion and preparing the body's machinery to make tears—then we get tearful ourselves. These mirror neurons are powerful, and it is in this complex interplay of brain mirroring that we can have a profound influence on whether or not someone else will experience anger. If we do not activate the mirror neurons that react to someone else's anger, perhaps we can prevent a full-fledged limbic rage in both ourselves and others.

You can imagine how this mirrored emotional connection could lead to significant increases in anger. And isn't this what happens so often? Think about the kind of facial expression that inspires your limbic response. It is usually an angry one with a message to back off and stop being a threat. As your limbic reaction activates your mirror neurons, your face is transformed to match the angry face of the other person.

But this natural brain response can instead be used in reverse. When your brain registers the other person's angry face, you are not required to mirror it. Instead you can use your PFC to activate the other person's mirror neuron system. When you project peace, that emotion and behavior could be mirrored as easily as the anger. You can make it your routine to project peace, whether it's directed toward your neighbor or a stranger at the grocery store. With her hundred-millisecond glance at you, it will be the first thing another person sees, and could have an impact on her decision to trust or be wary. When I approached the man putting the sign up on my lawn, I was activating his mirror neuron system. I could have influenced his brain to go limbic, but instead I influenced it to stay frontal. We parted as friends, not foes.

FROM REFLEXIVE TO REFLECTIVE

The process of imitation is more than just mimicry, according to German scientists at the University of Schleswig-Holstein who are studying human brain mapping. Their research demonstrated that imitation involves four steps. The first three are evoked watching another person do something—say, using a knife. First mirror neurons perceive the action. Second, they prepare you to perform and execute the action, and third, enable you to remember and then retrieve the action from working memory. If mirror neurons were solely about this type of mimicry, then the adage "Monkey see, monkey do," would fit perfectly. But there is more to it, according to Menz.

Seeing another person use an object also stimulates the brain to consider other options for how to use that same object. Menz and his team refer to this fourth component as "object affordance," and note that it is a late part of the brain activity he and his team measured. Your brain is weighing how to use the object and what will possibly happen if you do. This comes into play when the action perceived actually suggests another action.

For example, you see a knife; the object affordance might be to cut your veggies, whittle a piece of wood, or use the knife as a weapon. This important distinction extends the mirror neuron function beyond simply observing an action and preparing to mimic it. Object affordance suggests that mirror neurons have also sent their information to the PFC. The premotor mirror neurons may indeed be about "mindless mirroring," but the information they send to the PFC evokes the anticipation of future potential consequences of one's actions.

If I see a knife, I have choices in regard to how to use it. If I see a doorknob and my brain anticipates grasping the doorknob to open the door, I am using my PFC to anticipate the consequence of my actions. Whether I choose to open the door or leave it shut will be influenced by what I think I will find behind it. Don't we do this when we open a door to a relationship? Won't we be less likely to open that door if we think there is danger and anger on the other side, but more likely to do so if we have been calmed, are peaceful, and are beginning to trust?

Yet it is precisely because we do not blithely trust, because we are mostly realists and not just Pollyanna optimists, that we don't just imitate everything we see and open every door without wondering what is on the other side. Beyond our mirror neurons, the brain also has evolved other, highly sophisticated mediating systems. We must have evolved the ability to suppress the automatic mirror neuron response, as imitation is not always appropriate or safe. And you will not be surprised to learn that this inhibiting component lies in the PFC. A team of Dutch neuroscientists looked at intentional versus automatic imitation. They showed that it is the PFC that sends those "Don't do it" signals to the premotor cortex, effectively stopping the automatic response suggested by our mirror neurons. The study is compelling because it reveals the ability, built in and evolved, of the PFC to override the limbic reaction.

Naturally, this makes evolutionary sense. Early humans who just acted automatically, without at least some alternative reasoning, probably did not fare as well compared to those who were less impulsive, more cautious, and more analytical. Seeing an angry face might have made you angry, but if the automatic reaction was to act impulsively and aggressively, it could lead to serious injury or death. What would have led to an increased chance of survival, however, might have been recognizing anger in the "V face," retrieving memories that connected that face with past danger, anticipating results of your own reflexive reaction, anticipating the retaliatory response of the person who had originally signaled you with the angry face, and then using this knowledge to suppress your original automatic mirror response. The use of your frontal lobes to anticipate the consequence of your actions led you to survive another day.

Today it's still important to take note of the separation of automatic "Do it" and practiced "Don't do it" or inhibitory responses and to shift from an involuntary brain to a voluntary one, from a reflexive brain to a reflective brain. How can you apply this to your own anger control? When you do not respond to another person's anger with anger, you don't add fuel to his limbic response and can begin to modulate or change his emotions. By recognizing rage in another person, you can modulate it through respect and the projection of peace. You activate a different set of mirror neurons and begin to defuse the other's anger.

Exercise: Zero In on Anger

In each of the following scenarios, your mirror neurons might be activated by the person with the limbic reaction. But your PFC has the ability to change that instinctive, automatic response. In each of these instances you have the opportunity to go limbic or keep it frontal by using your PFC to project peace.

What would you do?

1. Your teenager slams her bedroom door and screams, "I hate you!"

    A. Yell back at her that she's spoiled and out of control.

    B. Tell her she's grounded for the next ten years for her disrespect.

    C. Say nothing and go make some herbal tea.

D. Wonder what she is so mad about and remember that soon she will stop hating you, but will probably never stop loving you.

The best answer is D. Your daughter is way out on a limbic limb. Because she's a teen, this angry impulsive outburst may occur more than once! The teen brain is still developing and maturing, following the course of evolution we discussed in Chapter One. So even though she may seem at times to be a miasmic amalgam of a temper-tantrum-prone two-year-old with the vocal chords of a fifteen-year-old, her actions are really a result of her limbic system working harder and having more influence than her PFC.

Even though this too shall pass, probably by the age of twenty-one, you can begin now to shift your daughter's brain back to the PFC through your own actions. Mirror neurons and your own wondering about whether she is envious or suspicious can lead to a great conversation and connection. Not right now while she is limbic, though. But you can begin the process by staying peaceful and respectful. Your own projection of peace may not work right away, but going limbic yourself will definitely not help and is likely to make matters worse. Use your own projection of peace to catch the attention of her mirror neurons. Let her know that you respect her time and respect that she is angry, and let her know that you care. Do not say, "I'll talk with you when you calm down." All that does is fan the flames of fury. She may interpret such a statement as a sign that you see her as out of control and that you have more control. This can activate the envy side of anger, and off she goes again. Instead, remain peaceful, let her know that when she is ready to talk, you will be ready as well. Mirror calm for her, and when she calms down, discuss what you can do together to redirect that anger to work for both of you.

2. A woman in line in front of you is yelling at the clerk and slowing down the rest of the line.

    A. Say nothing.

    B. Angrily tell the woman to just take her problem elsewhere because she's holding up the line.

(*continued*)

    C. Go to another line.

    D. Politely ask them both if there is anything you can do to help.

Again, D is the correct answer. Although the risk in this scenario is that you seem like a busybody, the way you approach the conflict can create a platform from which peace can prevail. The customer is in limbic mode, and the clerk may be right behind her, but his position and the adage that the customer is always right may be advocating that his brain remain at a PFC level. This can be hard when one's limbic survival mode is being so tempted to explode. But the clerk is outsmarting his own anger by treating the customer with respect, and is thus able to stop from simply launching into a limbic rage with the slightest provocation. The customer, however, is angry. You know that this means that she is either envious or suspicious of something. Perhaps she is envious that the clerk has power, and he is functioning as an extension of the store, which has wronged her. Or perhaps she is suspicious that her needs will not be met and that the clerk will take from her an opportunity for justice. At this time, she fights her battle alone, but likely would welcome an ally. The clerk may be looking for an ally as well. And lo and behold, here is a peacemaker.

When you politely offer help, you are projecting peace, subtly activating the mirror neurons of both observers. Your calm imparts that at least someone is not envious or suspicious, and not angry. You are also offering your time as a resource and building trust. Your presence sends a message to the angry customer that she is valuable and not alone, which can begin to calm the limbic reflexive perception that the situation is dangerous. You are also signaling the clerk that he is not alone either. You serve as a buffer and a potential bridge, and you are modeling how conflictual interactions can be managed with peaceful negotiation in which everyone wins, rather than through angry attacks where there are no winners.

3. In an important staff meeting, one colleague interprets your comment as critical of his department, and challenges you to provide a response in front of the others.

A. Address his comment calmly by saying that you never intended to be disrespectful, that you and he share the same concern.

B. Tell him to send you an email and you'll set up a meeting to talk about it.

C. Tell him that you're in charge here, and you can't address every insecurity among the group.

D. Ignore him as though he were insignificant and did not exist.

The best answer is A. Address his concern that you are encroaching on his resources, residence, or relationships, and appreciate the envy or suspicion embedded in his challenge, by showing him the respect he's requesting (by offering a polite response promising action). Project peace by acknowledging his anger and reassuring him that your intention was not to be critical. If you have a team at the meeting that is cohesive and trusting, it may be worth the time to check in with other people to hear their responses. If they thought you were critical as well, you have learned something about your presentation. You can then apologize to the injured party and assure him again that you intended no disrespect. If they think you were not critical, you have found allies, and the group can help calm your colleague so that you can all get on productively with the meeting. An angry brain is not the most creative problem-solving brain. However, if you do not have a trusting team, this strategy can backfire, and the colleague may think you are just further challenging his value as part of the group, which will only aggravate his anger.

In each of these instances, someone else's limbic system has been activated. In all three examples, you have intersected with that person on a personal level; in the last two examples, on the public level as well. You can try to use these opportunities to connect, decrease anger, build trust, and project peace. When you model these behaviors enough, other people will begin doing them as well. I have seen this on a daily basis in my program. Projecting peace can be contagious.

HIDDEN IN A HORMONE:
A KEY TO TRUST

Mirror neurons tell us a great deal about how our hardwiring equips us to project peace or to wage war. But along with this wiring are brain chemicals that reinforce our ability to project peace and build relationships with others. This is especially the case when it comes to the building of trust—a critical step in projecting peace. One brain chemical in particular—oxytocin—has emerged as a topic of active and productive research by scientists across the world. Oxytocin is a critical component in our ability to bond, connect, and trust.

When a person has a feeling of trust toward another, his or her brain releases this important chemical, which is actually a neurohormone. (A hormone is a chemical produced by one part of the body that has an effect on a different part of the body. Because oxytocin is a hormone produced by the brain, it is called a neurohormone.) It is oxytocin that sends a message to start the uterus contracting in childbirth. It is also associated with social behaviors like love, sex, and generosity. The more oxytocin released, the stronger the bonding between humans. One implication of stronger bonding is a reduction in stress: if I have someone to whom I am connected, I can rely on him or her more to have my back in times of need. It is this chemical that gives you that great feeling inside when someone says "Good job" or "Great piece of art" or "You are amazing." Because of this remarkable role in social connection, oxytocin has been called the "affiliation" or "cuddle" neurohormone.

In a recent experiment examining this correlation, scientists at the University of Szeged in Hungary gave sixty healthy volunteers, all strangers, a task in which they had to share secrets, a measure of intimate trust. They then measured the participants' blood oxytocin levels. Oxytocin is the chemical involved in trust: an attachment of one person to another. As expected, the oxytocin levels were higher in people who were able to share their secrets. Trust means that you feel part of a group, and as part of a group, you enjoy the safety of that cohort. In the second part of the experiment, the volunteers performed a mental arithmetic stressor test after which they again had their blood levels of oxytocin measured. In previous studies, such a test increased levels of stress hormones.

The results confirmed what researchers suspected. After taking the mental arithmetic stressor test, the oxytocin levels were no longer elevated, but had primed the body in a remarkable way: the researchers found that the participants' skin conductivity, as measured by cold sweat levels, and all the automatic body reactions expected in response to stress *were not happening*. The stress response had become "habituated," presumably by the prior elevated levels of oxytocin.

Habituation basically means that the brain and body are ignoring a stimulus. For example, if you live near a railroad, the loud and annoying sound of the train passing by will be very distracting at first. But over time, it becomes just an annoyance you ignore and then not even notice. Oxytocin seems to do the same thing for our brains and bodies: when you feel trust for and trusted by another person, stress is easier to handle. If you are not experiencing stress, you are significantly less likely to ignite the bomb of anger.

In our everyday lives, we do not choose the moments when we find ourselves in those trust or not-to-trust scenarios. Yet we do have influence over the instant impressions we make on people. In two basic ways, we can help another person's brain release oxytocin in order to build trust in us. One way is through obvious trust cues: the external impression we instantly give to others. The other way is "nonobvious": the subconscious impressions we project to others that come from our own long-formed thinking patterns. As individual survival machines, we have evolved to depend on other people, on groups, to enhance that survival. Most of the time, we are not even consciously aware that we are constantly assessing whether we are welcomed or are at risk of being banished. And as we have all evolved basically the same brain, we are all making similar ongoing assessments. This means that each of us has an influence on whether another person will feel welcomed or at risk of being kicked out of the group.

The PFC processes information so quickly that we may not even be aware that we were thinking anything at all. All we become aware of is the resulting limbic emotion those thoughts have generated.

What you think then affects what you feel, and what you feel can influence the impression you make on what someone else thinks. How do you project this critical message of acceptance or rejection to another person? Are you indeed welcoming, or are you standoffish and rejecting? The other's brain is assessing for these features all the time, and knows the difference!

The Obvious Trust Cues

Because the obvious is what most brains notice first, let's look at the impact of these impressions on people. As you read, think about how you react to someone who breaks these rules. Also take notes on how you could make some adjustments in your own current approach. In Chapter Four we spoke about eye contact and appearance in general as capable of decreasing suspicion. But they also enhance trust. The first obvious cue expands on the importance of eye contact in our world of electronics. Next we explore the influence of our appearance in a world where we are surrounded by strangers. In fact, there are several other things you can do in attempting to increase the oxytocin levels in another person, a few of which are offered in this section.

Make Eye Contact

"The eyes are the mirror of the soul." Eye contact very often puts a damper on anger, and face-to-face contact itself can defuse the potential for aggression. This is not an insignificant point. With the proliferation of PDA and cell phone devices, eye contact is becoming rarer. How many kids would say to another kid's face what they are willing to say on Facebook or in a text message? How many of us would swear at another driver if he or she were right next to us, face-to-face and in arm's reach and not encased in metal? How is this relative geographical barrier of our Internet generation contributing to the stress, anger, and mistrust in our societies? Eye contact has the word "contact" in it for a reason.

In fact, when a person is unaware that eye contact is important, the result is heartbreaking. This is the case with many people with autistic spectrum disorder or Asperger's syndrome. Unaware that eye contact is important, they avert their eyes and create anxiety and mistrust in another person who expects a different behavior and connection. Without intending to, kids with Asperger's can find themselves in a barrage of anger directed toward them with no clue as to how they got there.

Be Clean

The brain is designed to make a quick assessment of what it sees. A lot of evolutionary currency has gone into the ability to detect parasites. Animals infested with parasites were probably less able to ward off disease and were at higher risk for contaminating those around them. People who take care of their grooming appear less likely to have parasites and are therefore more acceptable to someone else. If "parasites" are detected, you are less likely to be asked to be part of the group and will then feel rejected and less respected. Just the suggestion of common critters like head lice or bedbugs makes you want to scratch. When you project an image of being unclean, you are more likely to trigger disgust than trust, no matter how sincere and trustworthy you are.

In some cultures, the way you smell has an impact on how you are perceived. Many people feel revulsion when they think that another person hasn't washed, implying that he does not take care of himself. In the United States, to smell good is to smell clean, and vice versa. Deodorant is a multibillion-dollar industry. Teenagers in particular learn quickly that how we smell will have a bearing on whether we are accepted by or rejected from a group. People who have urinary incontinence or irritable bowels may shy away from social situations, the fear of losing bowel or bladder control and the concomitant odor it produces being too embarrassing and shameful to bear.

In fact, a self-perception that you have a foul body order has even been given a clinical name: olfactory reference syndrome. Researchers in Rhode Island assessed the self-perceptions of a group of individuals in regard to their various bodily odors. These unfortunate people, 60 percent female, thought they had bad breath or smelled sweaty. The fear and self-loathing were so profound that remarkably, almost 70 percent of these people had thought about suicide, and 32 percent had actually made a suicide attempt. In most modern cultures, we take cleanliness and how people perceive our hygiene very seriously indeed.

Look Safe

When you look safe, the other person's limbic system is less likely to be activated, and he or she is more open to having a prefrontal, empathic impression toward you. Your appearance has an influence on another person's brain.

Wear Nice Clothes

Consider clothing a display, communicating to another person a part of your character and values. Our brain is designed to make a quick assessment based on these outward appearances, and when something is "off" in the clothing area, it opens the door to doubting a person's character.

When I was a medical resident, I tried a personal experiment. For several months, I wore a tie with my top button unbuttoned and noticed the way my patients related to me. For the several months after, I kept my top button buttoned. The patients seemed to respond differently. Perhaps I just liked having my button unbuttoned, but it seemed to me that the appearance gave off a more relaxed impression, and my patients seemed more open. These days, however, my wife informs me that I look less professional with my unbuttoned look, so when I go to a meeting or give a lecture, I button up. In that setting, someone who looks more professional may be seen as more credible and trustworthy. But with my patients, I still like the unbuttoned approach, because being trustworthy may be communicated by seeming more relaxed. In other words, be selective about what you wear depending on the situation you find yourself in. After all, you would not go to a job interview in your pajamas, but your kids probably wouldn't wear a suit to a sleepover.

Being trusted carries a huge advantage. If someone trusts you, that person is more willing to share resources, residence, and relationships with you, and you then have more access to these valuable survival commodities. Trust gives you a better chance of being part of an in-group rather than being placed in an out-group. So looking trustworthy is another important aspect of projecting peace.

Every detail counts when we are trying to garner trust and project peace. A recent study by psychology researchers at the University of Warwick in the United Kingdom confirmed as much. Study participants watched video samples of various individuals acting as "reporters," some with a trustworthy and others with an untrustworthy appearance. Subsequently, the participants were asked to recall which

TRUSTING BUT NOT GULLIBLE

We've been learning about the oxytocin-trust connection. But oxytocin is not just an "elixir of trust," as some might think. Although trust does elevate oxytocin levels, this increase does not make someone completely nondiscriminating and gullible.

Does oxytocin override cues that another person is untrustworthy? Researchers at the Université Catholique de Louvain

(continued)

(Belgium) designed an experiment to answer this question. In their recent study published in *Psychological Science*, a journal of the Association for Psychological Science, volunteers were to play a money game with partners described to make some seem reliable and others unreliable. Volunteers would play the same game with a "neutral" computer. Before the game started, each volunteer received a nasal spray of either oxytocin or a placebo and then played the trust game, with the following rules: "Each participant assumed the role of investor and could transfer money to a 'trustee,' in whose hands the funds would triple. The trustee would then transfer all the money, part of it, or none of it back to the investor. If the investor entrusted the trustee with all of his money, he could maximize his profits if the trustee was reliable and fair. Conversely, he could lose everything if the trustee was not fair. The trust game is perfectly suited to establish the investor's level of trust (i.e., the higher the trust, the higher the transfer)."

Would oxytocin cause an indiscriminate giving, suggestive of gullibility?

It may not have come as a surprise that the results showed that the players who received the oxytocin were more trusting of the computer and the reliable partners. In fact, they offered more money to the computer and the reliable partner than did the players who received the placebo. But when the players assessed who the potential unreliable partners were, the oxytocin effect didn't hold up—the players were not generous toward a potentially unreliable partner, regardless of which nasal spray they received. Oxytocin is a trust chemical, not a gullibility chemical.

As powerful as oxytocin may be, the brain is much more powerful overall, and before giving up valuable resources, it heeds the limbic emotion of suspicion to prevent the person from making a potentially foolish mistake.

reporter provided each headline and to assess the accuracy of the reports. The results of the study showed overwhelmingly that appearance highly influenced the believability of the reports given by the untrustworthy-looking reporters.

The Nonobvious Trust Cues

When we project peace, we are doing something that is both very complex and very simple: we are acknowledging the emotional experience of the other person. We accept his or her emotional state; we do not resist it or judge it. Referring back to the opening story of the chapter, the aggressive expression on my neighbor's face as I approached him signaled suspicion toward me. He perceived my approach to him as a threat. By acknowledging his anger and not responding to it with a retort or insult, I was showing him that I was safe and not a threat. What I did was no magic trick. Quite simply, I showed respect.

Showing someone respect is indeed a nonobvious, but probably the most powerful, method of building trust and projecting peace. This is a critical observation: When do you get angry with someone who is treating you with respect? You don't. The brain is not wired this way. You get angry when you want someone to change what he or she is doing: to start doing something or to stop doing something. But being respected feels great. Why would you want to change that? So when you feel respected by someone, you don't want that person to stop. You don't want him or her to stop treating you with respect. So you don't get angry.

Think for a moment about how you handle the limbic reactions of people close to you—your kids or elderly parents, relatives, or friends with whom you interact closely and frequently. If your child has a tantrum at the grocery store, as kids are prone to, do you lose control and start yelling at or hitting your child? Probably not (I hope). The same goes with your relatives and friends. You acknowledge their limbic reactions, not with your own limbic reaction, but

THE FACE OF TRUST

Take a look at yourself in a mirror. The human face has thirty-three muscles, allowing you to contort your face into hundreds of combinations, each one related to expression of the seven basic emotions. It's pretty easy to do those seven, so make a face for each: anger, surprise, disgust, fear, joy, sadness, and contempt. But when you try to express trust and make your face look trustworthy, what happens?

Although trust has been called the opposite of disgust, it's difficult to manufacture an expression that immediately telegraphs trust. This is because trust is not a simple emotion; it's a more complex brain "decision" based on assorted criteria that the brain processes unconsciously and instantaneously. In this chapter, we are examining both the obvious and nonobvious criteria for trust. When deciding whether or not to trust someone, your brain will instantaneously process both obvious and nonobvious information.

with acceptance of what they're feeling, with respect. This makes sense in our close relationships. We don't have to worry about trust with those folks. They trust us, and we trust them. The oxytocin is already flowing nicely.

The respect approach also works with strangers and people with whom you don't yet have a trust relationship. Showing respect establishes instantly that you are not a threat. Why do you wave with an open hand and not a fist? An open hand sends a message to the other person that you are not carrying a weapon and are peaceful. The person does not need to be envious or suspicious of your intent.

Shaking your fist at someone provokes a very different, limbic response.

Being respected makes you feel amazing. Being respected implies a positive connection to someone else who sees you as valuable. If you are valuable, you are less likely to be kicked out of the group to fend for yourself in a dangerous world of predators. You get to stay as part of the in-group.

Perhaps you have also experienced a limbic reaction that was defused by respect. If you've ever had a problem with your computer and found yourself on the line with a customer service rep, you can tell that the person on the other end of the line has been trained to remain respectful no matter how he or she is being treated. Hearing a respectful and helpful tone is very reassuring for many customers and can slow or even halt a limbic expression.

Customer service professionals have been trained to treat everyone respectfully and courteously and to be sympathetic to the customer's experience. And when they, or we, show respect to someone, we do this most effectively with another nonobvious behavior: absolute calm.

If you were to ask my patients or colleagues to describe me, I think they would all use the words "calm" and "respectful." And by being calm and respectful I am also calming, and eliciting respect. This is based on two things: the power of mirror neurons and the phenomenon that you don't get angry with someone you really believe is treating you with respect. When a patient sees me as respectful, it actually calms his or her brain. In our program, we work with teenagers who struggle with addictions to drugs and alcohol, and we have used the approach of remaining calm and showing respect to defuse angry outbursts that could lead to dangerous situations. Being calm is being peaceful, nonthreatening, interested, attentive, and without a need to take control or enforce power. (If you feel a need to be in control but are not, you are going to become anxious, but you can't leave the situation and flee. Instead, your anxiety will switch to anger, to get the other person to change what he or she is doing. The other person, however, can easily go limbic when faced with an angry brain approaching him or her. Two limbic brains rarely have a positive outcome.)

When I keep it frontal and remain calm and respectful, I influence another brain to also remain calm and respectful. What is especially encouraging is that our kids learn to do the same thing. Our program serves many troubled teenagers—some from good homes, some from dangerous neighborhoods, some with histories of unbelievable abuse and neglect, some stuck too young in the criminal justice system. And yet the culture of our program is one of respect and peace. As of this writing, we have been open for three-and-a-half years; we have treated more than eleven hundred unique patients, with an average of sixteen patients per day, which translates to over twenty thousand patient days. Even with all these patient-patient and patient-staff interactions, we have had fewer than fifty physical fights. Projecting peace, staying calm, and using the power of respect really do outsmart anger.

Staying calm goes hand in hand with showing respect in the non-obvious category of ways to project peace. When we stay calm, we are in PFC mode. We are resisting the urge to go limbic. Following the definition we explored in Chapter One, which stated that anger is an emotion designed to change the behavior of others, why would someone faced with a peaceful person want to change that?

SPECIAL CHALLENGES IN PROJECTING PEACE

As we all know, staying calm is easier said than accomplished in a limbic world where dangers are perceived and anger easily engaged. With this constant stress comes a lot less calm and less use of our PFC. Chronic stress has been shown to inhibit clear judgment. This was the finding by psychology researchers at the University of Wisconsin who designed a study examining the impact of stress on neurological processing of stress and on performance. Their results showed that at certain levels, stress and anxiety shift the balance of attention away from PFC-directed tasks to what they called "sensory-vigilance mode," which is governed by the amygdalae and other threat-sensitive regions—in other words, the limbic system. What this study showed is that acute stress appropriately activates our survival mechanism, increasing our attention and awareness of threats. But over time, we begin to tend to misinterpret information around us—ignoring things that are important and becoming distracted by things we misinterpret as potential threats.

The core findings of this research go beyond telling us that we're distracted by stress. That seems obvious. What isn't obvious is that when we are stressed and distracted, we are more likely to misperceive the world and to make mistakes. Our limbic system has been responding to threats automatically for hundreds of millions of years and is doing a good job protecting our survival. But it may also be partly responsible for critical misperceptions of people and the world. And what you perceive is what you think. What you think impacts how you feel. Staying in PFC mode and keeping it frontal can be an ancient evolutionary challenge for everyone, especially when stress is involved.

One of the remaining difficulties in reducing limbic responses like fear and anger is our deeply ingrained and diverse perceptions of what defines a trustworthy-looking person. This issue cuts across many lines—societal, cultural, racial, sexual, even political—and it cannot be addressed easily. Although our brains have evolved to be advanced and complex, their development is based on the foundations of having to survive. It's taken millions of years for our brains to get to where they are today. But those first two "ice cream scoops" are still part of us, those parts that are hundreds of millions of years old. What can we do with such a diverse structure, and how do we exercise our last scoop, the neocortex, and that "cherry" of a PFC? Think about your own perceptions and experiences.

How do you respond when you see a person in a wheelchair, her body contorted by some crippling condition? What about a man with bloodshot eyes and wearing dirty clothes, who is asking for handouts?

In less time than a blink of an eye, we make assessments—usually based on appearance—of the people we see, as to whether they are trustworthy or whether we should avoid risking any of our resources, residence, or relationships by interacting with them. Although we know we can't judge a book by its cover, the cover nevertheless has enormous influence on how we judge.

This process of discrimination, as natural as it is, inherently keeps people from seeing the better part of many others—and from projecting peace where and when it's needed. Our evolution has pushed us to be biased, to believe that our resources, residence, and relationships are being threatened by the person next to us. Instead, that person could become a resource, a member of our residence, a new and productive relationship.

Let's look at a typical situation. Very often, through no fault of their own, some kids get acne in their teen years. It's possibly the most dreaded side effect of adolescence. Acne is so visible, and humans so quick to assess, that we make strong assumptions about the character of the person based on something that is literally only skin deep. In a recent study, University of Miami psychologists surveyed 1,002 adults (eighteen years old and older) and 1,006 teenagers ages thirteen to seventeen, and asked them to compare pictures of adolescents with and without acne. In the second part of the study, the same adults and teens were asked to evaluate their own experience with pimples. Among both the adults and peers, 40 percent of kids with acne were perceived as being shy, 25 percent as nerdy, 22 percent as stressed, 22 percent as lonely, as well as various percentages of boring, unkempt, unhealthy, introverted, and rebellious—all just because they had pimples. The study found that 64 percent of teenagers who had acne felt embarrassed by it, and 55 percent felt that it was the single most difficult part of being a teenager. More than 70 percent of teens with acne had lower self-confidence or shyness; other problems included difficulty finding dates, problems making friends, challenges at school, and trouble getting a job. Adults and peers both felt that teens with acne were also more likely to be bullied.

But for those kids with clear skin, every one of those problems seemed to fade away. Both the teens and adults rated this group higher on every favorable characteristic. We see someone with acne, and a flood of thoughts goes through our mind. Sometimes we feel sad for the person, because on some deeper level we think it must be horrible to have acne, aware of how much that person will be judged, sometimes to the point of being shunned or bullied. We recognize that they have been exiled from the in-group and assigned to an out-group.

Acne is just one of a myriad of examples of how we often mistakenly misjudge a person's character. Look at the billion-dollar industries that address not just acne but clothing, teeth, and plastic surgery. In many countries, outward appearance carries enormous significance, which creates and feeds these massive industries. But our reliance on basic appearance also makes a huge statement about what we value in others, at least when we use "beauty" as a measure of inner, hidden values, such as morality and ethics. We so easily mistake a caricature of a person for the character of that person.

The reliance on outer appearance creates an insidious and potentially lethal danger. Because our brain is designed to compare sets of data, we consider the people with whom we identify in comparison to the people with whom we don't. This leads to the menace and threat of a world viewed through a lens of in-groups and out-groups. Racism, sexism, ageism, classism, and religious intolerance all stem from this basic, primitive, yet still prevalent inclination to lump people into groups and clusters: you are like me; you are not like me.

If you are not like me, perhaps I need to consider that you are a threat to my resources, residence, and relationships. If you are not like me, am I at risk? Do I engage envy or suspicion? If you are not like me, can I trust you? Will you try to take what I have, or do you have more than me? Are you at an advantage, an advantage I may need to correct? And just because you don't look like me, does that preclude us from sharing our resources and residence, building a strong and mutually advantageous relationship? These are all questions to ask ourselves when trying to project peace.

We would all like to think we have control over these impulses. But as irrational as it sounds, even decisions as important as voting for a president are influenced by our primitive limbic response. All presidential candidates dress in particular ways to appeal to certain groups. But electability is also profoundly influenced by gender and appearance. Northwestern University researchers asked a group of men and women to judge the electability of hypothetical male and female political candidates. The survey, which was based on appearances only, asked if the candidates were competent, dominant, attractive, and approachable. Although all voters were likely to select a person who appeared more competent, the male candidates most likely to win votes appeared more approachable. But among the female candidates, it was those who were considered more attractive who were preferred. Not surprisingly, men were more likely to vote for attractive female candidates, whereas women were more likely to vote for approachable male candidates.

Most of us are unlikely to run for president, but the findings are still important. If you are a male, being approachable is an advantage. This makes sense. After all, who would trust or want to approach an angry, scary-looking person? When you project a peaceful, competent persona, other people are more likely to want to be around you. And if you can gather people around you, the chances increase that you will be successful. You have expanded your in-group with access to more resources, residence, and relationships.

So what can we do to calm that limbic urgency to judge? A big step may be simply to accept who we are and how our brains work and then to use this facet of our humanity to influence what the other person thinks. Although it may not be your fault if you have acne, it becomes your responsibility. Same goes if you're running for office. This may not seem fair, but how you look has an impact on how you are perceived and thus how you make others feel. And if you project an appearance or attitude that stimulates envy or suspicion, you run the risk of activating anger in another person.

Remember, no matter who you are or what you look like, other people will not get angry at you when you treat them with respect. By projecting peace, you create a relationship in which the other brain can find a way to begin trusting you. If you do not appear as a threat, and present yourself as approachable rather than as someone to avoid, you have a greater chance of being able to move into the next step of calming another person's brain. You can now begin to wonder what that other brain is thinking or feeling and what is important to it—to let it know that it is valuable. You will begin to engage empathy, the subject of the next chapter.

CHAPTER 6

Engage Empathy

The great gift of human beings is that we have the power of empathy, we can all sense a mysterious connection to each other.

—Meryl Streep (1949–)

I am human: nothing human is alien to me.

—Terentius (c. 190–160 BC)

Charlie dreaded getting on the school bus. He waited at the end of his driveway, about to relinquish the safe haven of home. His mom watched from the kitchen window as she did every day, waving goodbye and giving him a thumbs-up of support. He waved back, trying to smile. The broken rumble of the bus preceded it around the corner before the big yellow carriage rolled into view.

The doors peeled open, and thirteen-year-old Charlie carefully climbed the three steps, greeted Mr. Jones the bus driver, and moved down the aisle. As usual, no one offered a seat, and he made his way to the rowdy section in the back. The torture began as soon as the bus started moving again. "If it isn't crater face!" yelled Bobby, who reached out and knocked Charlie's hat off his head. After he did that, he pulled Charlie's hair, stopping only when he thought Mr. Jones was looking back in the mirror. Bobby's taunt was a regular occurrence that the rest of the kids seemed to ignore.

Reading this or just about any story about a defenseless kid getting bullied probably gives you a feeling of dismay, sadness, even a twinge of anger. This is empathy. You share in the feeling that you know

Charlie is experiencing. His injury is the constant bullying. The insult is that nobody seemed to care. If you were bullied yourself in your past, tough memories can resurge, perhaps even with a wish that someone had helped you. If you were never bullied or teased, you may remember seeing this happen to someone else, perhaps feeling too powerless yourself to intervene.

But what if the story had ended like this: one day, a pretty classmate turned around and asked Bobby, "Why are you so mean to him? He didn't do anything to you." Bobby mocked the other kid, but he was stopped in his tracks by a very reasonable question.

The classmate becomes a hero in this story and in our imaginations, because she expressed what we were all feeling—empathy for someone who was experiencing hurt—and had the will to act on it. Many people express regret that at some point in their lives they lacked the courage to say something when they could have touched another person through their empathy. But among all those kids, on that one day, only this girl had the courage to act on her empathy for Charlie.

Remarkably, even very young children are able not only to feel empathy for another but to *engage* empathy—to anticipate the thoughts of others and how they may worry about their own resources, residence, and relationships. Just as we explored in Chapter Five, Projecting Peace, it is this enhanced anticipation of another person's feelings, be it suspicion, envy, or pain, that prepares *us* to create the outcome we want.

Although we cannot exactly "read" another person's mind, we *can* gauge his or her feelings through our innate ability to empathize. With this information, we can then influence that person's emotional experience, as well as actions. When we actively engage empathy, we are paying attention to what we perceive other people are feeling. This perspective taking can ultimately help us better negotiate business relationships; manage friction with our spouse, kids, and friends; and navigate our way through daily human interaction with less anxiety and more confidence.

EMPATHY AND VALUE:
IN THIS BOAT TOGETHER

When the girl spoke up for Charlie in the school bus scenario, it became a powerful and influential moment. By engaging empathy, the child crossed a threshold into what is fundamentally the shared human experience. Her empathy became an instrument of anger modulation, changing the very outcome of Charlie's ride, his day, and the days or lives of a few other kids on that bus. When you understand this and engage your empathy, and even when you see someone else engage empathy, you feel galvanized by it. You also feel more connected to the people around you. Why is this?

I believe that at the core of who we are as human beings is the need to feel valued by another human being. Think about this in your own life. As a child, you want to be valued by parents. As you grow older, you want to be valued by friends and teachers, and eventually a life partner. You also want to be valued by your own children, their friends, potential in-laws, and the world of people with whom you have contact. In fact, we want to be valued even by complete strangers. Feeling valued helps us feel safe and calms our limbic fears of being alone and winding up as a predator's meal.

When you treat another person with respect, you are acknowledging his value, which enables him to contemplate trusting you. Hold open a door for someone, let someone with a single item go before you in the grocery line, don't interrupt when another person is speaking, give an elder a seat on the bus—these are all forms of conveying value and respect to others in a civil society. This trust opens a metaphorical door, reducing someone's potential for anger caused by suspicion or envy, because you have allowed her "in" by valuing her. She is likely to reciprocate and value you as well.

I live in a town with a very busy main street. Every morning it is a challenge to make the left out of the coffee shop driveway, which requires crossing the stream of traffic. I sit there becoming more and more irritated and frustrated as car after car drives by either oblivious to my wish or purposefully speeding up to delay my exit. I can feel the cortisol and adrenaline coursing through my body as I try not to go limbic.

But when a driver slows down, flashes her lights, and gives me the signal that she will pause long enough for me to drive out, a different feeling develops. In her small way, this complete stranger has empathized with my perspective and let me safely cross the road. I am much more inclined to let another car cross in front of me later that day, which shows how this simple empathic response can reproduce itself, allowing me to impart value to another stranger. But we cannot know how or when to convey value to others without the ability to feel and engage empathy.

THE ROLE OF THEORY OF MIND IN RELATIONSHIPS

Engaging empathy is more than being polite and neighborly— although those are ways of expressing it. Empathy has its primary home in the brain, within the middle part of the PFC, technically called the medial PFC (see Figure 6.1). This brain area also houses a family of other cognitive functions that include a person's perception of his own bodily state, emotional judgments, and ability to assess and attribute meaning to others' behavior. Brain lesions or growth delays in this area lead to interference with a number of behaviors, including empathic processing. In fact, autism spectrum research has focused on this relationship, as children with disorders like Asperger's syndrome are known for their inability to anticipate others' feelings. Lacking this ability tragically cuts them off from the core of how human beings interact with each other: a fundamental interchange of information driven in part by the use and development of our PFC. But in the average developing brain, empathy, like speech, is an aptitude that develops naturally through humane and caring interaction from the moment of birth.

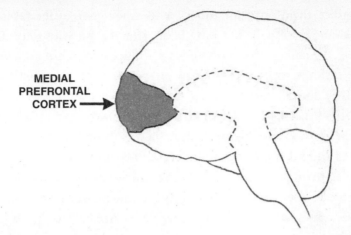

MEDIAL
PREFRONTAL
CORTEX →

Figure 6.1. Medial Prefrontal Cortex
Illustration by Sophia T. Shrand.

Before empathy forms, however, the underlying ability to appreciate what someone else is thinking or feeling is required. As noted in earlier chapters, scientists call this awareness theory of mind (ToM). The concept was first introduced by psychologists David Premack and Guy Woodruff in 1978. In their groundbreaking study, they were investigating whether chimpanzees could attribute intent or mental state. They had the chimps look at video of a human actor struggling with various problems like being locked in a cage, not being able to reach food, or shivering from cold. The chimps were then given photographs of the solutions to each of these problems, and consistently selected the correct remedy.

That study opened up a field of research on how, when, and why humans have developed the ability to assign mental states to ourselves as well as others. The classic example used to explain ToM is called the Sally-Anne task or test. Children being given this test are told or shown a story of two characters, Sally and Anne. Sally has a basket, and Anne has a box. Sally also has a marble. Sally puts the marble in her basket, then leaves the room. While she's gone, Anne takes the marble and puts it in her box. Soon afterwards, Sally returns. In the test, the child is asked where Sally will look for her marble. Very young children typically respond by saying that she will look in Anne's box. They don't understand yet that Sally still believes that the marble is where she left it, as she had not seen it being moved from her basket to Anne's box. The young child cannot take Sally's perspective or point of view. Indeed, from the young child's point of view, if he or she knows it, then everyone knows it. The child's perspective is the same as everyone else's, and everyone else's the same as the child's. A child that says Sally will look for the marble in Anne's box has not yet developed ToM.

Two-, three-, and four-year-old children are just beginning to form ToM, or the ability to understand that Sally's thinking is separate from Anne's and that their own thinking is separate from everyone else's. By the time children are six and seven, they are more likely to respond by saying that Sally will look in the place she left the marble—in her basket. By this time, they are fully aware that another person has her own distinct thought process and are able to make predictions of that person's behavior.

Without thinking about it consciously, most people assume that everyone has the ability to take another person's perspective, to have an active and intact ToM. In real life, however, there are many variations among individuals. Being around someone with an impaired ToM can make people feel uneasy. We expect someone to be interested in what we are thinking or feeling. When he is not, we get very anxious, and even angry, because we want him to change and to *care* about what we think or feel. Interacting with a person whose ToM is intact and engaged is more likely to calm down our own brain. We know that he knows we have our own thoughts and feelings and that he is interested in them, which is the basis for the development of empathy.

The lack of ToM becomes very obvious when we observe people who have not developed this ability. This isolating experience is the core deficit in such conditions as autism, and the cruelest loss in those suffering from dementias, such as Alzheimer's. These folks may display behaviors that seem insensitive, lacking in interest or concern for others. But what we know is that these people are not being oppositional in response to your feelings. Rather, they are oblivious to your feelings. Until you know that they are not doing this on purpose, but have an impairment in their ability to appreciate your own thoughts and feelings, you are going to get mad. But once you know, it can actually stimulate empathy in you, as you become aware of how alone and isolated their disability has left them.

HOW EMPATHY FORMS

As a child's ToM develops, there will be critical experiential and learning moments, especially in regard to the way the child is being treated by his or her caregivers, which will help develop a child's innate capacity for empathy.

Imagine a three-year-old boy playing by himself in the sandbox with his toys. Gradually a feeling, slightly uncomfortable, starts in his belly. For a moment it goes away, and he again turns his attention to his play. But then it is back, a little stronger, and stronger still. He has felt this before, and he knows what to do. The child leaves his sandbox and finds his mother in the house. "Mommy, I'm hungry," he says. "You're hungry?" she replies. "Then I'll feed you."

What has happened here? The child has identified a feeling that he thinks may be hunger. It's in his belly, a little uncomfortable, but he's felt it before, and it went away with food. Any food. Still not quite old enough to satisfy the discomfort himself, he has gone to his mother, a person who has taken care of this problem before, sometimes even before he knew he had the problem.

He doesn't ask, "Am I hungry?" He makes a statement and then waits for confirmation. "You're hungry?" asks the mother. "Then I'll feed you." The child is now saying to himself, "Yes, this *is* hunger. I thought I was hungry, and my mom said she would feed me, so I must have been hungry. OK." He catalogues the feeling of hunger for future reference.

In this simple example, the power of empathy is evident. He thought he was hungry, his mother confirmed he was hungry, and then she fed him. She listened to him, wondered about how he was feeling, and was not dismissive. He did not get angry, despite being uncomfortable and hungry. He did not worry that he would not be fed or cared for. His experience was endorsed, his needs nurtured, and his value validated.

This type of simple interaction can have a lasting effect on how a person engages in his future attachments and his ability to be empathic toward someone else. As he gets older, the types of attachments he makes at school, with friends and romantic partners, with employers and employees, will have as part of its foundation interactions such as these: if you are hungry, I will feed you. When a need as basic as hunger is met, the individual's biological barometer is set as one of a person who sees himself as valued and respected. In the vast majority of homes, this simple interaction follows the same path. "I'm hungry." "You're hungry? I'll feed you." All three of the R's have been addressed: resources were made available in the form of food; the setting and environment of his home (residence) was confirmed as a place of safety, nurturing, and comfort; relationships were strengthened in his interaction with his mother.

This simple and ubiquitous scenario, one that happens millions of times every day in every part of the world, powerfully illustrates how empathy is tied to another's need. The typical, healthy response would be the response the child received—respect through validation of the request, and the offer of food, an altruistic expression.

Yet there are many times when a parent cannot immediately meet the needs of the child. Sometimes a parent may say, "You're hungry? OK, I'll feed you right after I finish what I'm doing." By asking the child to wait without invalidating the child's experience of hunger, the parent has been able to interact with the child in a way that models mutual and reciprocal value and respect. "I will feed you because you are hungry, but I have confidence in you that you will not die of starvation in the next five minutes and that you can tolerate the discomfort of hunger without resorting to disrespectful and unsafe behaviors." Although the child may remain hungry for a few minutes, this response also enhances the child's self-concept as his mother confirms that she sees him as a person who can be patient for the greater good.

In fact, this delay of gratification can exercise the PFC, but only when the anticipated promise is fulfilled. The child is learning to anticipate the consequences of his actions and to anticipate the actions of others. When the mother does indeed feed him in the near future, he will begin to solidify a trust and belief that events in the future are likely to have a good outcome. But another important experience has happened to the child. The mother has asked him to wait.

In this example, the initial acknowledgment from the mother—confirming the internal experience of the child with an external validation—is powerful. She has communicated an understanding of his invisible internal state. But by asking him to wait until she is finished, the parent has also asked the child to appreciate her own internal point of view, to have empathy toward her. By engaging empathy with her child, the mother models an ability to engage empathy with someone else—an essential step in learning how to appreciate and influence others' emotions as we grow into adulthood.

When you engage empathy with someone else, you give her a chance to become interested in what you think or feel as well. You can both begin to feel more valuable. Feeling valued leads to trust. In turn, the feeling of trust reduces the other person's anxiety and potential for anger.

Exercise: How Well Do You Engage Empathy?

Most people think they're empathic, but how do you really rate? How often do you do the convenient thing but not the empathic thing? Which is really the "right" thing to do? Engaging empathically with someone else is always a good thing. Think about how you respond when you know someone really cares about what you're thinking and feeling. This behavior spurs desire for interaction from a position of respect. You can learn to consistently engage empathy and increase the chances of a positive outcome in any situation. Take a moment to review the scenarios that follow. Put a square around your limbic response. Then put a circle around your frontal decision. Do you see how your action will influence the feelings of the other person and the potential outcome of the dynamic? Think about how you and everyone involved will feel an hour after the incident.

Example 1

It's early in the morning, and you're en route to work via train when the man next to you spills some of his coffee in your lap.

You

A. Scream, "You idiot! I can't believe you just did that!"

B. Remain silent, ignore efforts to help you clean up, and immediately go to another, drier seat.

C. Accept apologies and assistance sincerely and say, "Hey, accidents happen. It's OK."

How would you want someone else to react if *you* had accidentally spilled the coffee?

Example 2

You are driving to work and a car cuts you off, then continues weaving in and out of traffic ahead of you.

You

A. Think, "What a jerk" and hope he gets into an accident.

B. Speed up to follow him with the intention of cutting him off in glee.

C. Wonder if he has an emergency, such as a wife in labor about to give birth in his car.

When you shift your perception of intention, you can approach that person with a different attitude, usually more empathic. Don't you think differently about that guy when you wonder why he is cutting you off?

Example 3

You've worked twelve hours, but come home to find your eldest kid freaking out because she has a term project due the next day and needs a piece of poster board.

You

A. Tersely tell her that she should have thought of that before you got home, and you're not going back out.

B. Smartly tell her that she should have planned better and not waited until the last minute.

C. Sigh, then tell her that you're exhausted, but that you will send her other parent out to get the poster board.

D. Sigh and go help your kid.

If you're lucky, you might be able to choose option C, as your partner might engage empathy for your sake, but if not, I trust you'll choose D. This is the real task of engaging empathy: looking at things from another person's perspective. When you shift out of your own limbic system and into your PFC, you're better able to regard and treat the other person with respect. We all have thoughts and feelings churning inside us, constantly evaluating our surroundings: assessing for danger, safety, alliances, predators, and more. When the other person perceives you treating her with respect, it calms the limbic part of the brain. Respect is the great modulator of anger.

Empathy shifts your brain into a much more logical and compassionate assessment process. Developing this tool is a way to shift away from your

(continued)

own anger and begin to decrease the anger of another. You can appreciate someone's point of view, how he worries about his own resources, residence, and relationships. Rather than be a threat to any of the domains, you can begin to build an alliance between the two of you, turning your anger as well as the other person's anger into power and positive action. Once you have shown you are not a threat, the limbic system calms down, and you have two people in PFC mode, mutually respectful and ready to cooperate.

EMPATHIC SOCIETIES: WHAT HUMANS DO FOR ONE ANOTHER

So why is empathy so vitally important between individuals and within society? The answer to that question can be found in the opening story of this chapter. Which bus would you want to take or to have your child take? The bus where bullying is happening because it is tolerated by everyone or the bus where it is not? When people engage empathy, they are more relaxed, cooperative, trusting, productive, creative, and happy. People feel more connected to one another and are therefore much more likely to help each other. And societies where people help each other are much more likely to thrive.

EMPATHY VERSUS SYMPATHY

No louder shrieks to pitying heaven are cast, when husbands or lap-dogs breathe their last.
—Alexander Pope (1688–1744)

There is perhaps no better way to explain the difference between empathy and sympathy than to look at the feelings associated with the loss of a pet. It is a unique kind of loss, especially when the pet was long lived and greatly loved. This is simple to grasp if you've ever been a pet owner. The sudden absence of a loyal, loving beast can sting for months. If someone you know loses his family dog of many years, you will feel very clear empathy toward this person and his loss. You've walked in these emotional shoes. When you feel empathy, you understand and feel another's feelings as if you were experiencing them yourself. You "get it" and may be more likely to send a "sorry for your loss" card or a little extra support to someone whose experience you closely understand. You acknowledge *your* empathy for *his* loss.

If you have never experienced grief over a pet, you can still feel a supportive emotion toward a person you care about. This is sympathy. You are sorry for his loss, but don't truly understand its scope and depth. That said, a close friend who has a great deal of empathy toward others in general can be a strong support because she understands what another kind of loss feels like, and she can still "share" in a sense of sadness and hardship. She is not walking in the other's shoes, perhaps, but she can still care deeply. We cannot all have the same experiences in life, but when we're engaging empathy, we can still anticipate someone's feelings, whether we've experienced the exact same emotional suffering or not.

A broader difference between empathy and sympathy, however, has to do with the range of emotions they address. I don't think anyone would feel sympathy for a person who has just fallen in love, had a first child or grandchild, or landed a great job. Sympathy is confined more to an appreciation of another person's loss, rather than to acknowledging gain. Empathy involves one person's ability to appreciate the emotions another person is experiencing due to the circumstances in that other person's life. If I have had an experience similar to what you are going through and I can relate to it personally, that's empathy. This common experience has the potential to then bind the two of us together as you recognize that I understand and care what you are going through.

The idea of people helping others—acting altruistically—may seem somewhat contrary to the long established Darwinian notion of survival of the fittest. In fact, this is one of the conundrums of classic evolutionary theory. Why would giving to someone else at your own expense help you survive? How would such a behavior have evolved in human or other species? One theory is that the great modulator between self-interest and altruism is in fact empathy. In a recent study published in the *Annual Review of Psychology*, psychologists at Emory University asked the basic question, "Why did empathy evolve?" In their review, they concluded that altruistic behavior evolved for the simple reason that the performer of an altruistic act was motivated by a "return-benefit" expectation.

In other words, one altruistic act would have laid the foundation for the possibility of reciprocal altruism in the future. Empathy here opens the door to trust: I trust that when I am in need of a resource, residence, or relationship in the future, you will be altruistic toward me. I'll scratch your back; you'll scratch mine. I've got your back *now* if you've got mine sometime in the future. Trust becomes a statement not just about the relationship you have with someone here and now. It is anticipating the relationship five minutes, five days, five decades from now. We all know how hard it is to build trust and how easy it is to dismantle. Trust implies the promise of altruism, and altruism depends on empathy, an ability to discern whether you need help from me.

In this view, the classic Darwinian dogma actually is preserved: organisms perform actions to ultimately help their genes make it to the next generation. Altruism creates a relationship between two or more organisms in which the assistance of one today influences the assistance of the other at a future date. If this were not the case, and an animal that did something for another was not rewarded in the future, then the behavior itself would be less likely to be selected for and to advance genetically. It would simply die out because altruism would not have any survival advantage. Indeed, according to most evolutionary theorists, most species do not exhibit altruism when it comes to helping outsiders and nonkin, an unfortunate perpetuation of the in-group versus out-group survival position.

But luckily for us, both empathy and altruism have long prevailed in the genetic coding of humans. In fact, human babies as young as eighteen months have been shown to act altruistically without any kind of training or prompting. Studies by Felix Warneken and Michael Tomasello at the Max Planck Institute for Evolutionary Biology demonstrate that prelinguistic babies will voluntarily assist an adult, even a stranger, achieve a goal. In a fascinating series of videos, available on the Web, you can see a young child pick up a marker off the floor and hand it to the adult who was acting as if she couldn't reach it. In another experiment, the babies will open a cabinet for the grown-up who is carrying a pile of books. The man bangs on the door several times, and without prompting, the toddler walks over and pulls open the doors so that the man can place the books there. Writing in the journal *Science*, the authors explain that this behavior "requires both an understanding of others' goals and an altruistic motivation to help." We can't arrive at altruism without empathic abilities.

Think about your own experiences. You "feel" differently about a person who is generous than a person who is stingy. In fact, you are probably more likely to help out a neighbor who helped you before than the one who never lets you borrow his hedge clippers or that cup of sugar. Altruism creates a promise between people and may even exercise our PFC ability to anticipate the future consequence of our action. I do something for you today and may call on you to return the favor with a service in the future. For a behavior to have been sustained so globally across the human species, it must confer some enormous survival advantage. By enhancing the chances of success during times when resources are not as plentiful, altruism has become a highly selected-for trait and behavior.

EXPANDING OUR EMPATHY: FROM OUT-GROUPS TO IN-GROUPS

For thousands of years, humans have been locked into a competition for what appeared to be limited resources, residence, and relationships. Feelings and expressions of empathy and trust were reserved for those in your tribe, your in-group. Even today, our brains are compelled to make this distinction. Our ancient survival instinct demands that we sort through the differences among people based on the primal puzzle and question of whom we can trust. This one is my friend; this one is not. This is my religion; that one is not. This is my ethnicity; the other is not. This is my country; that one is not. We are constantly dividing and subdividing into in-groups, with which we identify, and out-groups, with which we do not identify and which we consider "different."

Unfortunately, these perceived differences continue to divide people, as we are less willing to respect, value, and engage empathy toward members of out-groups. Similar to other species, we are limbically less likely to demonstrate altruism to a group that is outside our perceived affiliation. Feelings of distrust and anger arise more quickly toward someone in an out-group. Driven by our limbic brain, anger can speed and spiral out of control if we do not use our PFC to filter and put a brake on primal feelings like envy or suspicion. When we cultivate differences between "us" and "them," we create the scaffolding for conflict and even war.

When other people, cultures, religions, and even political parties within the same country seem so different, how can we reach across these conceptual divides to expand our in-groups? By engaging empathy. There are far more commonalities in human life that unite us, and over time we have been discovering them. Perhaps one of the most compelling examples of this is Alcoholics Anonymous. The supportive discussions that began in 1935 between two white men in Akron, Ohio, struggling with alcohol have now expanded to millions of people across the world. Over twenty-one million copies of the Big

Book, the basic text for Alcoholics Anonymous, have been distributed worldwide. Cutting across every single cultural, ethnic, gender, and class divide, AA creates a fellowship, a responsibility for each other, and a sense of belonging. AA participants in practically every country across the globe have created an in-group united around their challenge with alcohol. This social connection, scientists believe, is what supports sobriety.

Psychology researchers at Massachusetts General Hospital surveyed 1,726 AA members over a fifteen-month period, investigating which factors helped reduce relapse and resumption of drinking. The researchers studied various aspects of AA members that could contribute to sobriety and relapse, including spiritual practice, self-efficacy, social networks, and feelings of depression, worthlessness, and guilt. They found that the social network itself had the largest impact in helping an AA member remain sober. When you start having fewer friends who are using and more friends who are sharing in the goal of abstinence, you stay sober longer. You have switched your values to a different in-group, in this case one that is more productive, constructive, and mutually beneficial. Being part of a group like this helps individuals decrease their feelings of depression, worthlessness, and guilt, while increasing their spirituality and religiosity. But it was not just AA as an abstract organization that helped the members stay sober; rather it was the fellow members of AA, who reminded them of their value to other human beings, believed in their ability to be sober, and made themselves available to support their sobriety. In so doing, these fellow members also maintained their *own* sobriety. Altruism toward another member of your in-group helps you survive better yourself.

The fellowship of AA creates a sensation that is the opposite of what many alcoholics experience in society at large, where they often feel vilified and rejected as immoral substance abusers and failures. Indeed, it is possible that this clear message—"You are now cast out of our in-group and are on your own"—may itself contribute to the anxiety and distress experienced by many people who struggle with addictions, driving them further into their drug use to escape these fearful and isolating feelings.

But the simple, support-based solution that Bill W. and Dr. Bob discovered in 1935 in Akron is a lot more than talk. All along, the fellowship of AA included a hidden, neurochemical component: oxytocin. AA is thought to succeed for many in the treatment of alcoholism because of the release of oxytocin in individuals who feel accepted, connected, trusted, and safe.

But of course oxytocin is not confined to AA. Oxytocin is the neurochemical that binds us to each other in general, at home, at work, or across an expanse. The release of oxytocin we experience when connecting to a person sitting in front of us also extends to helping others far away. In-groups don't have to be in the same town. We have seen evidence of how social media have enabled people to engage empathy on a global level, whether it be through supportive Twitter feeds to young revolutionaries in the Arab Spring; the dissemination of YouTube videos showing injustices throughout the world; or innumerable websites, blogs, and Facebook pages that help raise money for those in need after earthquakes and other natural disasters. And our need to extend empathy appears just as vital as our instinct for anger. Anger has been around for millions of years, and it's not going away anytime soon. But empathy can help alleviate our innate anger triggers by enabling individuals to embrace "differences" and unite into ever-widening in-groups.

Our growing awareness of this desire to connect, and our means and ability to connect with others through social media, offer an unprecedented opportunity for humanity. We have a natural inclination to engage empathy when we perceive injustice and pain, and this ability may be changing our evolutionary path. Ultimately, I believe, empathy may be even more powerful than anger and the forces that encourage the formation of out-groups. On both an individual and global level, engaging empathy allows us to nurture and encourage one of the greatest and too often untapped resources of our planet: our unlimited human potential.

CHALLENGES TO EMPATHY

As humans we are all susceptible to stress, fatigue, and obstacles in getting what we need every single day. In our most vulnerable moments, we are at risk of abandoning empathy toward others. You know from your own life that, depending on your state of mind, you are more or less likely to let someone pull in front of you, give a street musician some spare change, help your kid with homework, or even enjoy yourself. In fact, scientists have found that when we are experiencing high levels of stress, we are less likely to laugh at certain types of jokes or even to comprehend them. Researchers at Stanford assessed responses of fifty-six participants who rated comprehension and funniness of three types of cartoons. They found that among members of the higher-anxiety group, their ability to enjoy jokes based on assessing the mental state of others—their ToM—was compromised.

This shortcoming also appears to have its origins in our evolutionary past. Under perceived stress, our limbic-activated brain sends us signals that our immediate survival is in danger, so why be altruistic and start worrying about what someone else is thinking? But today, waiting that extra minute at the stop sign or at the grocery store is unlikely to leave you as prey for a saber tooth tiger. Your PFC is capable of thinking this through and advising the limbic brain to relax.

Our ability to engage empathy can also be compromised when we feel that our ability to act would have no impact. This phenomenon was the subject of research by psychologist Paul Slovic, who has studied what lies behind the "psychic numbing" that occurs when people are confronted with humanitarian crises, such as food shortages and genocides, in faraway places. Studies show that groups like Save the Children are able to raise more money when they feature an individual child's story, for instance, instead of talking about the wider problem of a country. Our empathy and compassion for single, identifiable "victims" extends even to animals. Think of the hundreds of pets that had to be abandoned during Hurricane Katrina. Yet it was the image of the lone barking dog on the rooftop that inspired legions of animal lovers to descend upon Louisiana to rescue and find new homes for these animals. But empathy is stoked less, according to Slovic, by news reports of seemingly intransigent problems that feature "numerical representations of human lives which do not necessarily convey the importance of those lives." He points out that numbers represent cold statistics, "human beings with the tears dried off," that lack feeling and fail to motivate action.

Even on an individual-to-individual level, sometimes it is challenging to remain empathic, loving, and caring, especially if you are not receiving that same feeling in return. Perhaps the most poignant example is the emotional burnout caregivers experience when giving care for extended periods to those with chronic medical conditions or Alzheimer's. Burnout occurs both for family members who care for their loved ones at home and for medical staff who tend to the needs of patients in nursing homes. And the burnout itself leads to feelings of guilt and then anger at the sense of being powerless in the face of the relentless progression of disease, especially one that robs the patient of the capability even to recognize the person offering care. In fact, in many people with dementia, ToM (empathy) is devoured as the PFC falls helplessly to the gnawing deterioration of cognitive and intellectual abilities. In being robbed of these critical PFC faculties, they are also losing their humanity, something the caregivers have to remind themselves of. The solution to this burnout? Care for the caregiver. Support from someone else, sharing the burden, removing the isolation, reinforcing the value, and ultimately engaging empathy and stimulating oxytocin.

Psychic numbing, feeling overwhelmed and powerless, can interfere with our ability to use our PFC to analyze the situation, make a plan, and anticipate the outcome of that plan. Sometimes empathy hurts too much. Trying to solve someone else's problem can be so daunting that we just want to get away from it all. That flight desire can arise at home, at work, or when trying to make sense of the complex problems and stress of our world. Sometimes we make the wrong choices about how to restore our psychological balance. And what is the so-called crutch that many people turn to when thinking they need to relieve stress? Drugs and alcohol, substances that can lead to abuse. The irony here is that substance abuse can decrease levels of oxytocin, leaving a person with a deficit in empathy, which in turn leads to other destructive behaviors: aggression, violation of other people's rights and property, being more concerned about the next fix than about fixing the relationships that have been damaged by drugs. No empathy there.

We see this type of cycle all the time in my program working with teenagers struggling with addiction. Our first step in trying to break this destructive cycle is to treat each person with respect. For instance, an out-of-control sixteen-year-old charged into my office one day, interrupting a meeting. My response to him was not "Hey, you're rudely interrupting; wait outside." Rather, I calmly asked him what was on his mind, listened, told him I really wanted to speak with him, and then suggested that he wait a few minutes just outside the door and that I would be right with him. It's true that his behavior was rude, especially for a sixteen-year-old. But I also knew that the boy was struggling with heroin addiction. When he felt listened to and was promised help, he could be reasonable and let the anger cool. By treating this boy and all the other kids with respect, we signal to them that they are valuable. When they feel valued, they can let go of anger more easily and are able to engage empathy in a deep way. They begin to recognize how their own substance use has had an impact on the self-value of their parents, and many can rekindle a relationship that had been sorely impaired by drugs and alcohol.

For many of these kids, surviving what they have been through has made them amazing empathizers. They understand rejection, negligence, abuse, and personal struggles more than many adults. In our program, they are praised and seen as valuable, and the cycle of oxytocin-driven prosocial behavior is started. They can begin to be supportive of each other's recovery and sobriety as part of their own restoration.

Addictions are not crimes, but can lead to them. But the real crime is turning our back on people who struggle with this (or any other serious concern), driving them away from our in-group and lumping them as bad, immoral, with no value, to be placed in an out-group, far away from us. This is certainly not the way to generate oxytocin or to help others.

RESTORING EMPATHY

Cultivating empathy with respect has proven successful among challenged kids in our program. Meanwhile, many other groups are looking at ways in which to nurture empathy among children well before they reach the teen years. In Toronto, Canada, the work of an organization called Roots of Empathy has been instrumental in showing that empathy can be developed in very young children, and even among older kids whose behaviors were aggressive and negative. They don't use any fancy equipment or photographs in the classroom. In Roots of Empathy, little babies become the teachers. Parent volunteers bring in young babies, usually starting around three months of age, and the kids all sit on the floor with them and observe the children's faces, sounds, and reactions. A trained Roots of Empathy instructor guides the monthly visits and explains what the babies are feeling and how they perceive the world in each developmental stage. They also help the kids understand what the babies need and how to take care of those needs. By observing the babies, kids learn how to identify and better communicate their own feelings, and in the process become more sensitive to the emotions of others.

Researchers from the University of British Columbia who have studied the impact of Roots of Empathy have found that the experience with babies measurably changes the observing kids' behavior. One study found that almost 90 percent of the kids who had displayed bullying behavior, what researchers call "proactive aggression," showed a major decrease in these behaviors after a year with the Roots of Empathy program. This compares to an astonishingly low 9 percent among kids who were not in the program. Milder types of bullying behaviors, such as gossiping and leaving friends out of group activities, were also measurably reduced.

Nobody knows exactly how this works, but neuroscientists suspect that the process of observing the babies alters the kids' brains and that oxytocin is at work. In the course of working together as a group, the kids are also rewarded with feeling plugged into and part of something communal—another oxytocin booster. In essence, the children are expanding their in-group. Once part of an in-group, you have a greater chance of receiving the benefits of altruism, with the hidden promise that at a later date you will reciprocate. It is much more desirable to be part of a group sharing resources, residence, and relationships.

Programs like Roots of Empathy are extremely important because they help increase the capacity for empathy in all children, not just the class bullies. Studies have shown that up to 85 percent of school bullying and harassment episodes go ignored by onlookers. This has an adverse effect on everyone. The bully on the school bus makes the ride to school stressful for every passenger, not just the direct victim. By engaging empathy, kids can learn how to support each other and also learn that taking action actually feels better than ignoring the plight of the picked-on kid. But what kids and adults all need help with is in how to put empathy to work.

Think about the first three steps in identifying anger. They involved introspection: recognizing rage, envisioning envy, and sensing suspicion. The next two steps, projecting peace and engaging empathy, acknowledge that we all have basically the same human brain; if I am feeling angry about something, chances are good that someone else is as well. When we project peace, we mobilize mirror neurons that shift the other person's brain to the PFC and away from the limbic system where anger is generated. When we engage empathy, we're utilizing our human intuition to consider how another person thinks or feels.

We all want and perhaps need to be part of a group. But if we continue to pit one group against another, we all ultimately lose. In his recent book *The Social Conquest of Earth*, E. O. Wilson suggests that our evolution as humans has involved a complex balance between our selfish tendency and our altruistic tendency. Within a group, it is easier for members to act altruistically toward one another than it is for them to do so toward members of another group. Groups that are altruistic also win out over groups in which the members cheat and are selfish: the first can cooperate to win; the second engages in in-fighting and can never get organized.

The problem we face as humans is the artificial division into different groups based on affiliations. The divisions can be large, such as between nations, or small, such as between a first-grader and a second-grader. They can lead to wars or to dismissive behaviors that your group is not as cool as mine. But there is another option: the recognition that, in reality, we are all one group, *Homo sapiens*—one enormous, highly diverse group of human beings ripe with potential. We have evolved an ability to use the modern, newer PFC to outsmart the more ancient angers, envies, and suspicions that threaten to keep us trapped in the dark recesses of our heritage. When we embrace that we are really one large group, each of us will have access to more resources, residence, and relationships. Instead of competing for the 3R's, we can cooperate to increase them and thereby increase our own success. Shylock of *The Merchant of Venice* had it right all those years ago when Shakespeare crafted the words, "If you prick us, do we not bleed? If you tickle us, do we not laugh? If you poison us, do we not die? And if you wrong us, shall we not revenge?" (Act III, Scene 1). Beneath the different colors of skin, we are each human. Beneath the different colors of skin, we each house an ancient brain ready to revenge a perceived wrong. Beneath the different colors of skin, in each of us lives a primal fear of being rejected and a primal desire to be accepted. The challenge to each of us is to expand our concept of the group so that we can all be more successful. Through projecting peace and engaging empathy, we each create opportunities to transform our world of strangers into a world of potential allies.

Challenges still remain, simply because we are, indeed, individuals. No matter how good we may be at sensing another person's perspective, we can't know for sure that our perception is accurate. In fact, how many times have you been disappointed in someone who you thought should have *known* how you felt but didn't seem to get it? How do you know what someone is thinking or feeling? You ask him. How do you let someone else know about your own thoughts and feelings? You tell her. We have reached a point in our evolution where we can truly listen and understand each other's point of view, with the shared goal of the survival and betterment of this very large group we call humanity. We can take our well-honed PFC abilities to the next step toward reducing anger and conflict when we communicate clearly, as discussed in the next chapter.

CHAPTER 7

Communicate Clearly

It takes two flints to make a fire.
—Louisa May Alcott (1832–1888)

*The single biggest problem in communication is
the illusion that it has taken place.*
—George Bernard Shaw (1856–1950)

For Kevin it had been a hectic day at the office. As he was finishing up, his wife, Jane, rang and asked him to pick up some milk on the way home. "It's been a crazy day, but I'll do my best," he told her. Having heard the positive-sounding tone in Kevin's voice, Jane built an unconscious expectation that she would soon be receiving the much-needed milk for the kids' dinner. But the store was closed by the time Kevin got there, and he arrived home empty-handed. His wife, who also had a stressful day at work, became upset and responded, "But you *said* you would get it." "No, I said I'd try," said a beleaguered Kevin. With two tired people who still had to get dinner for the kids, a tiny miscommunication was all that was needed to fuel the anger response.

This exchange could have several possible outcomes. You can imagine tempers rising and a vicious spat to follow. Or perhaps Jane displayed the cold shoulder of resentment, anger held inside. But I like to hope that Jane, using her PFC to recognize rage and engage empathy, replied, "We're both exhausted. The kids won't starve. Let's have dinner, honey." With those few words she would communicate clearly to her husband that nothing mattered more than the harmony between them.

Interactions like this take place every day, everywhere, and with everyone we know. With each interaction comes an opportunity to minimize the anger response of all parties involved and to create a positive outcome. Indeed, the need for thoughtful interaction actually becomes a responsibility in a healthy relationship and for a civil society to function properly. We must convey information to each other peacefully, respectfully, and safely. Without clear communication, we remain a civilization constantly in conflict and war.

Throughout the chapters in this book, we've been exploring how humans are interconnected by virtue of the shared wiring of our modern brain. We all experience limbic-system impulses like envy and suspicion, and we share the capacity for empathy. It is because of these evolutionary parallels that we are able not just to interact but to engage one another. And although we cannot control anyone, we influence everyone. The tools of this influence can be found in the many ways we learn to communicate.

One of the great hallmarks of humanity is language. What you say to people affects their feelings and thus their behaviors. *How* you say it is equally important. With good communication skills, you help the person with whom you're speaking become receptive to your thoughts and ideas. You disengage his fear, engender his trust, and engage his empathy. These simple actions bring both parties into what I call "primary PFC mode": a place where human beings function at their best, whether creating a science experiment, performing on stage, cooking a feast, flying aircraft, or building a monument. But to do these things, we need to communicate clearly.

YOU SAY "TOMATO": THE ELEMENTS OF LANGUAGE

When Jane heard her husband say "I'll do my best" in the chapter-opening story, she didn't hear just his words; she heard much more:

his intent, his positive tone, his shared need. In her ears, they all added up to the perception that he would pick up the milk. His actual words didn't seem to matter.

Jane's ability to detect the implication of her husband's words represents a remarkable feature of our brains, an ability that has developed over millions of years. As humans we have evolved an ability to rapidly decode the hidden emotional message in a person's voice. Our ancient hominid ancestors probably didn't have a word for "pull," for example. Just a sound or a sign. The word itself came much, much later. Spoken language as we know it is relatively recent. Written language even more so.

As scientists unravel the secrets of brain structure through the use of fMRI technology (high-resolution scans of actual brain activity), the mystery of the brain mechanisms that go into the production, reception, and processing of language is becoming clearer. As if on an archeological dig of the mind, brain scientists are gradually determining the precise pathways and neural connections that allow communication to happen. The growth and expansion of particular parts of the brain, such as the temporal and frontal lobes, occurred in lockstep with the development of language. In other words, language has evolved along with the actual configuration of the brain.

Over time, the human brain has been shaped to accommodate our need for survival. As we formed clans and primitive social networks, we began to find that *cooperative* interactions required *coordinated* actions. And the coordination of those actions mandated that I be able to let you know what I was going to do and that you would let me know what you were going to do. We needed to be able to interpret one another's actions, behaviors, and motivations. These abilities enabled us to pull together when we needed to, strengthening our efforts, or to assign different functions and tasks to get the job done. If we needed to kill a mammoth, it would have helped to coordinate when and where we would throw our spears. Pointing and grunting probably worked for a little while, but over millennia, human abilities advanced along with our capacity for language.

EAT YOUR FINGERS OFF

Decoding the meaning of words is a sophisticated process, one we often struggle with even within the same language. But add another language to the mix, and the risk for miscommunication can rise starkly and even humorously. Some of the greatest business blunders have occurred when American companies have exported certain products abroad without properly researching the impact of the local translation. For example, when Kentucky Fried Chicken tried to translate its classic slogan "finger-lickin' good" into Chinese characters, the unfortunate result was a plea for KFC consumers to "eat your fingers off." Coors beer encountered a similar challenge when translating its slogan "turn it loose" into Spanish. Would you really want to drink a beer that encouraged you to "suffer from diarrhea"? One of my personal favorites also involved a Spanish translation. When the pope was going to visit Miami, a region with a strong religious following among Hispanics, T-shirts that were meant to say "I saw the Pope!" (el Papa) instead joyfully announced "I saw the Potato!" (la Papa). And who can forget the classic Ford Nova? When exported to Mexico, it did not do well. No surprise: in Spanish, *no va* means "doesn't go."

In fact, language and mirror neurons were likely intimately connected as we developed our social networks. In the chapter Project Peace, we explored mirror neurons and their influence on actions and emotions. It appears that mirror neurons may also have contributed to the development of language. Michael Corballis, a professor from the University of Auckland in New Zealand and author of the book *From Hand to Mouth: The Origins of Language*, goes so far as to suggest that language "evolved from manual gestures, initially as a system of pantomime, but with gestures gradually 'conventionalizing' to assume more symbolic form." Mirror neurons likely played a pivotal role in this progression.

As language evolved, it incorporated all those facial and body movements that had previously been associated with guttural sounds. These days we continue to combine facial and vocal elements with language. Many of us use elaborate hand and arm movements to emphasize the emotions we now also communicate through words. Although sometimes culture specific, hand gestures carry meaning, and often elicit a similar gesture by the person who sees them. Someone waves at me; I wave back. Someone starts to shake hands with me and puts out her hand; I put out my hand in response. Someone makes an angry gesture with his finger; well . . . I try to get my PFC involved and not just my mirror neurons!

What we say now has an impact on what may happen next. As our brains became more adept at anticipating the future—inherent in the development of the PFC ability to anticipate the consequence of an action—language became a crucial component in communicating one's intent clearly to another human: let's go here to hunt; there's a mango tree in bloom over the hill; we should get there by tomorrow; follow me to a safe place to sleep.

But words are only a piece of the puzzle of communication. In all languages, the tone of the voice, the inflection, cadence, volume, and rhythm all enter into the communication of a person's feelings. Each aspect elicits its own response, an emotion or thought in the other person. It is the combination of these expressions that signals one's actual emotion, thought, and intention.

From as early as seven months old, infant brains become attuned to the emotion conveyed through voice. Using near-infrared spectroscopy, researchers at the University of London found that the voice-sensitive area of infant brains—the temporal cortex—was activated by emotional "prosody," or what is called the music of speech. Published in the journal *Neuron*, the study showed that when parents speak to their babies, it's often with prosody, meaning that they're not communicating information as much as making lilting sounds and words to convey love and assurance. Measuring the response in children's brains reveals that the intended prosocial communication is in fact achieved.

The effects of prosody are also achieved in adult brains. Studies have shown that whether a person is two or fifty-two, the brain will interpret tone of voice in exactly the same way. The words themselves may mean little, especially when conveying emotion. This is why even babies who have not said their first word will smile and coo when you talk with a warm and interested tone. The words you use are still meaningless to them, but the intention is received and understood.

Recently, investigators from China, the United States, and Portugal measured brain waves created when a person listened to nonsense words spoken with a particular intended emotion. They observed that the brain is configured to rapidly and efficiently interpret vocal sounds and intonations made to elicit a particular emotion, such that it can distinguish, for example, a happy voice from an angry one. Perhaps it goes without saying, but you can make this distinction yourself: the way we say something is just as powerful in modulating an emotion in another person as the words we use.

We also use visual information to interpret communication. Within the blink of an eye, we unconsciously assess a person's face and body. Is she smiling? Is her expression relaxed? Is she gritting her teeth? In fact, our brains are designed to match up particular sounds with particular facial expressions. In an interesting experiment at McGill University, psychology researchers showed that when people heard a phrase of gibberish (for example, "Someone migged the pazing") spoken in different ways, they could connect the way it was said with a corresponding face; they matched a fearful voice and facial expression with the most accuracy. This makes evolutionary sense: if someone else is afraid that a danger may be nearby, then I should be alert to this, to enhance my own survival.

Exercise: What Are You Having for Dinner?

As we've seen, it is not just words that activate your fight-flight mechanism. It is the way those words are said—the tone, the inflection, the rhythm. The way you feel about something deeply influences the way you say it or the way you hear and interpret what is said to you. Take this sentence as an example:

"I am having lasagna for dinner."

If you like lasagna, the sentence will sound one way, perhaps excited. If you don't like lasagna, it may sound quite disgusted. But try experimenting with emphasis on each word in the sentence. For instance, "*I* am having lasagna for dinner." Or, "I *am* having lasagna for dinner." Each time, you completely change the tone and thus the meaning of the sentence. Isn't it interesting how many different nuances you can find just through emphasis? Now try adjusting the cadence and rhythm. Make the sentence a question and try stressing the word "lasagna" or "dinner."

Now let's see how easy it is to influence someone else by using this same sentence. You can inspire jealousy by emphasizing the "I," which could telegraph that you alone are having lasagna. With the same emphasis on the "I," you could also make the person suspicious by implying that you are trying to take his or her lasagna. Try it yourself. Make the sentence a demand, a question, a joy, a sadness, a seduction. Amazing, isn't it? The way you say the words has just as much impact as the words themselves.

FINE-TUNED FOR COMMUNICATION

Whether we're interpreting sounds, tones, expressions, or rhythm, we're able to do all this thanks to our mirror neurons, those brain cells that mirror an observed action in anticipation of the need for imitation. Mother Nature is a fiscal conservative, frugal with her expenditure of energy. So, rather than there being completely different sets of mirror neurons, those very same cells that activate when you see another person reaching for a banana appear to be activated in communication between two humans. Scientists have found that mirror neurons actually enhance the communication between people. Psychologists at the University of Dundee in Scotland call this "reciprocal communication." It's almost as if our neurons are already in communication with another person's neurons—well before an expression or utterance is even made.

In the process of evolution, we rarely threw anything away. If a part of our body was not as useful anymore, rather than expend energy to get rid of it, Mother Nature merely did not attribute any additional favor or selective survival advantage to having it. Although there may be more to the appendix or little toe than we yet know, these parts of our body can be removed with minimal impact on our ability to survive. But in the same frugal manner, we have found ways to add additional functions to parts and chemicals we have already evolved. The mirror neurons involved in language are great examples. As we emerged as a social animal, it was enormously important to interpret the intention of another person's communication. And as discussed earlier, we used actions and sounds long before more specific words. But would we evolve different parts of the brain to accommodate auditory cues in addition to visual ones? Would it be cost-effective to expend energy to develop separate brain pathways for those functions?

In a recent fMRI study, Italian scientists from the Center for Cognitive Science at the University of Turin suggested that the answer is no. Instead, the same brain network that appears to activate for language and gestures also conveys the meaning and intention of those gestures. The interaction between the person expressing and the one interpreting those expressions represents the musical dance that occurs with every interaction. We watch the body and face even as we listen to and process the words, tone, and prosody of another.

These neurons are also put to work in decoding written communi-cation. Humans are unique in this capacity. When we use the written word, our brain adeptly perceives a collection of ciphers through a visual mechanism: the eyes. Right now, your brain is interpreting visual data, which consist of contrasting pieces of dark lines against a white background reconstitut4ed into shapes and patterns: letters, words, and sentences. We have agreed on a conventional use of commas, periods, and other punctuation to create a rhythm and flow to the sentence, also translated by your brain. The period at the end of the previous sentence and the capitalized letter after it created a slight pause in the flow and cadence of the ciphers, which your brain inter-preted as a need to pause, just as it did now, following that last comma. And did your brain startle when you read "reconstitut4ed," thinking, "Hey, a typo. That 4 doesn't belong there"? In fact, the proofreader of the book originally got to the word and corrected it before reading this sentence and learning that it was intended.

Through the many sophisticated ways we communicate, from spoken to nonverbal to written, modern humans are finely tuned and designed for clear communication. Yet in spite of highly advanced biological and technological tools for communication, we remain shackled by the context in which we try to interpret a communication. You hear "Surprise!" very differently when the lights suddenly come on in a darkened room and people start singing "Happy Birthday" than if you hear the same word coming from your daughter when she is telling you she is going to get married to a guy about whom you are not too sure.

THE NEEDS OF COMMUNICATION

When I communicate with you, I am trying to get across my own emotional or cognitive state, or I am trying to respond to yours. Also, sometimes when I communicate with you, I may be trying to change your emotional state, your cognitive state, or both. For instance, I understand that you are sad, and I want to cheer you up; I'm in need, so please help me; I like this political candidate, and so should you. Each communication puts forth a need or a response to a need of some kind. The quality of my emotional or thoughtful response to your need will determine the degree, level, and quality of emotion I generate in you. If you respond with anger, this will likely bring up anger in me. If you respond with peace, this will likely make me more peaceful. We all do this in our interaction with each other all the time.

Remember, anger stems from a perceived threat to a resource, residence, or relationship—all fundamental human needs. If someone makes a comment about how attractive my wife is, my relationship might feel threatened if I wasn't too sure how things were going between my wife and me. Or if someone I didn't know well asked for a large financial loan, I would feel the need to protect my resources. A simple disagreement can turn into a brawl when one party perceives a threat to his or her respect, or sense of being "right," which fits into one's pride or "residence."

To a large degree, we want our communication to elicit a positive emotional exchange. Although we cannot always meet a person's need, we can use empathy to allay the anger response by listening to and acknowledging that need. This is practicing and conveying respect. How would our homes, communities, workplaces, governments be different if we always treated each other in a way that acknowledged another person's needs? But humans are imperfect beings, swayed strongly by emotion. When swept up with feeling, two parties most often fail to communicate. Even when only one person becomes angry, compromise and negotiation can break down. If you've ever tried to calm or persuade an angry person to work with you and communicate along rational lines, you know how challenging this can be.

How well do you do when you try to negotiate out of anger? How well *can* you do if you are going limbic instead of keeping it frontal? Negotiating out of anger treads a fine line. If you are angry, the person with whom you are negotiating realizes that it is going to take more to appease you and close the deal than if you are being sweet and nice.

Considering that anger is an emotion designed to change the behavior of someone else, sometimes showing you are angry may indeed get you what you want. But this strategy can backfire, according to a study published in the *Journal of Personality and Social Psychology*. Researchers from the Netherlands found that an angry person can be deceived more easily by the person with whom he is bargaining, resulting in his getting much less than what he could have bargained for had he not expressed so much anger. They also found that some of the angry people actually didn't get to make a deal at all, especially when the person he was trading with just stopped negotiating because the angry person was trying to bully her into making a deal for too little. Sometimes it is just not worth trading with an angry person, so the whole business is called off. In both cases, the angry bargainer winds up with either way less than he could have or nothing at all.

As explored early on in the book, anger can be a powerful and compelling emotion, part of who we are and how we became successful as a species. But anger has a cost, and sometimes that cost can be too high, depriving us of resources, residence, and relationships. Being angry doesn't help you get what you want because you are not thinking as carefully about how to get it as you might otherwise. The PFC is responsible for strategy and planning, then anticipating the consequence of your actions. If you are going limbic, you effectively deprive yourself of a major strength and tool in bargaining. But when you and the other party are in primary PFC mode, you can respectfully come to a place where you can "agree to disagree" and move on to higher ground and greater good.

In the chapter's opening story, Kevin showed up without the milk, and Jane had a limbic response. But Kevin's tone and body language projected peace. Ultimately, Jane read these signals, could see there was no attack on her resources or residence, and decided that milk was not something to get angry over. These are decisions we come to so rapidly that we are not even conscious of them. But when we reflect on the success of this approach to keeping unnecessary conflict out of our lives, it increasingly becomes an essential routine for all of our relationships. With practice, we can turn our instincts into a technique.

You have learned how to promote peace by looking peaceful, but you also have to sound peaceful. Using an angry tone only alerts the other person that she may be in danger, and activates her limbic response. In my practice, I have found that talking with a relaxed, calm, and respectful tone eventually results in decreasing the anger of a rageful teenager or psychotic adult. I have witnessed tens of thousands of occurrences where an angry brain is calmed, but not by my responding back in fear or anger or by freezing. Rather, I believe I am activating a fourth response to threat, something that may be unique to humans, and that is friendship.

STOP, LOOK, AND LISTEN: THE FOURTH F

As a child psychiatrist, I am not unused to having a crying, angry, and hysterical teenager in my office. If I were to try to influence her with words like "Please control yourself" or "Losing your temper won't help things," I would not make much progress connecting. These are responses that shift away from the friendship response and into a limbic mode where communication shuts down. She may get angrier thinking I am dismissing or trying to change her feelings.

Instead I may ask, "What are the tears for?" or "Sorry for being Captain Obvious, but you seem heated." Rather than dismiss the emotion, I acknowledge the emotion and express an interest in why and how it got there. I convey that I am much more interested in why she is feeling what she is feeling at that moment than in trying to change her behavior in that moment. I might say, "I am a psychiatrist, not a judge. I'm simply interested in why people do what they do," to let my patients know that I view them with respect and interest. I project peace, use mirror neurons, engage empathy, use ToM and oxytocin, and create a foundation of value, trust, and acceptance. In this capacity, I do not have any impulse to go limbic myself and can stay PFC focused.

But we are not psychiatrists in our day-to-day activity with the vast majority of people in our lives. Instead, we are often strangers interacting with other strangers. We have developed the capacity for trust, for friendship, as an elegant, productive, and remarkably effective alternative to fight, flight, or freeze.

TALKING *TO* OR TALKING *WITH*

When we communicate clearly, our active listening conveys our interest in, valuing of, and respect for the other person's point of view. When we are not dismissive of a person, we do not activate his or her flight-fight-freeze response. Instead, we activate what I call the friendship response built on the pro-social, reciprocal communication of an interactive fellowship, or "in-group." One simple way to begin to achieve this reciprocity is to recognize how often we say "talking to" instead of "talking with." My patients will comment on how nice it is to talk to their mom or dad, and I will observe that they have actually been talking *with* their mom or dad. Talking *to* someone is talking *at* him or her. It is unidirectional. You may know people who do this. Often you feel as if they're delivering a monologue about themselves. But talking *with* someone is a dialogue, a reciprocal communication, a fellowship of friendship. When you talk *with* someone, you have a better chance of communicating clearly together and building a stronger foundation of trust. Trust leads to a sharing of the 3R's, and everyone winds up more successful. *With* trumps *to* every time.

In friendship mode, we can recognize rage, project peace, and engage empathy. We can let the person know we are interested in him and then communicate that interest with a calm, unhurried voice. Think how successful you have been in the past when you tried to command a person as to what to do or how to behave. Compare that to the times when you initiated communication and became an active listener.

In my treatment program, I utilize a technique I call "Stop, Look, and Listen." This simple technique applies well beyond the walls of a clinic. It is an approach that each of us can use every day in every conversation should we so choose. At home, at school, at work, at the shopping mall—by listening, we can communicate fundamental emotional messages like empathy, trust, understanding, and love. This works for children and adults alike, and can be crucial when trying to keep channels of communication open with teens and young adults. Listening to a person's thoughts and feelings, no matter how young she is, is treating her with the respect she deserves.

Taking the time to stop, look, and listen communicates clearly a message of value: I am placing on hold my primal drive to forage for a resource that would benefit me, by offering to you my time and attention. This is the communication we send to another person when we let him know we are interested in who he is and what he is feeling. Stop, Look, and Listen sends the message that the other person is respected and valued.

Stop, Look, and Listen can apply to all your communications—with your friends, your colleagues, your in-laws, your boss, your children, or anyone with whom you come in contact. When you're listening, it's vital to keep it frontal yourself so that you can identify the possibly limbic need that is being communicated—just as I do with the often limbic outbursts of my patients. When the person feels that you've listened and that you respect her, your empathy and interest in her can curb or calm her potential for a limbic response. As varied as all our communications are throughout the day, in each scenario, we have the opportunity to keep our relationships running smoothly, actively aiming to reduce anger and conflict when they begin to emerge. You can apply this technique to each of the following groups.

Couples

If you've ever been or still are one half of a couple, married or not, then you know well that two people cannot agree on everything. Being in a romantic one-on-one relationship can become a pressure cooker when both people have busy, separate careers and social circles they want to maintain. In the early stages of relationships, our "love"-inspired brains are flooded with oxytocin. No conflict is too great that we cannot forgive. Communication seems so easy in the beginning for the very reason that we are trying really hard to accommodate the object of our great affection. With our brains filled with joyful chemicals, we operate in primary PFC mode where affection and respect go hand in hand. There is no possible threat to any of the 3R's: we bask in the unlimited resources of a fertile relationship within a safe and relaxed residence. A partner who knows that you will be there for him or her can more easily let you go off and work.

Although the honeymoon stage abates in many relationships, our ability to communicate clearly and in a healthy way does not have to. But when it does, couples can be in danger. Think back again to Kevin and Jane's exchange over the milk. Kevin communicated verbally that he tried. His body communicated that he felt bad, and he did not act defensively at Jane's charge. At that point, Jane and Kevin's communication could continue along one of three trajectories.

Poor communication. Jane stayed in limbic mode, attacking Kevin and not respecting his effort. Her response signaled to Kevin that he was a failure and that she disapproved of him. She effectively shut down communication between them. Jane did not stop, look, or listen. Instead, she went limbic and was trapped in her own fight-flight response. She interpreted his inability to produce the resource of milk as a statement that her needs, and the needs of the children, did not matter—that he perceived them to be without value. She got angry because she wanted him to change, to do something different.

Anger response. Once Jane communicated anger toward Kevin, he became angry in response. He had tried his best and was offended that Jane did not acknowledge his effort, instead focusing on his inadequacy. He began to feel that she saw him as without value, and his own limbic fight-flight response was activated. Kevin became angry in response to Jane, his own mirror neurons being activated. She had wanted him to change and recognize her need; now he became angry and wanted her to change what he perceived as putting him down. There were now two angry brains in limbic mode, with the chance of clear communication ever more distant.

Communicating clearly. Jane recognized her own rage, but also Kevin's effort. She stopped, looked, and listened. The tone in his voice expressed genuine remorse. He felt that he had let her down, an affirmation that he saw her as valuable. She observed that he felt bad, and she engaged empathy as her own mirror neurons activated. Very quickly, she backed down from a limbic response as her primary PFC took control. Rather than go limbic and activate fight-flight-freeze, she kept it frontal, activated friendship, and embraced their relationship and mutual effort to meet the needs of the family. In response, Kevin's empathic mirror neurons also activated. He apologized for not getting the milk, and offered to go out now and pick some up. This gesture reassured Jane further as to his commitment to the family, and their value to him. With the foundation of projecting peace, the two could use ToM to engage empathy, shifting both their brains from a limbic reflex to a primary PFC reflection. This allowed their now calmer brains to communicate clearly, leading them to share their resources, residence, and relationship so that they could both be more successful. This is yet another example among many of how we control no one but influence everyone.

In the first case, Jane did not use Stop, Look, and Listen. She let her limbic response take over, treating Kevin scornfully and with contempt. Indeed, many studies have shown that couples who communicate from a position of contempt have worse marriages and much higher divorce rates than couples who communicate from a positive position of affection. Confirming common sense, researchers at the University of Delaware were able to predict newlywed marital outcomes based on two interaction contexts: contemptuous or noncontemptuous interactions. The couples who engaged in contemptuous communications, or those in which one would make a demand resulting in the other withdrawing, had higher rates of divorce than the couples who had more positive ways of dealing with conflict, based on a foundation of love rather than contempt.

Contempt is dangerous because it conveys reluctance to share any of the 3R's. If I am in contempt of someone, I perceive her with disgust and view her with disrespect. Why would I want to share any of my resources, residence, or relationships with her? But as I become more aware of this and recognize that my partner also holds me in contempt, I become suspicious that the person will try to take from me, or envious that she has me trapped and has power over me financially, and that a divorce would cost me much of my 3R's.

It may be more cost-effective to stay in an unhappy and unhealthy relationship. But instead of fight or flight, I will freeze and try to make myself invisible by staying late at work or going out to nighttime meetings. My limbic system will be in high gear and my body flooded with cortisol, leading me to seek relief from this stress-infused marinade. The brain wants to feel pleasure, and if we have to choose between pain and pleasure, we will choose pleasure every time. If we cannot get the prosocial, healthy oxytocin pleasure of being in a relationship where we feel valued, we will find pleasure elsewhere, anywhere, even in the isolating world of drugs and alcohol. The pleasure from an internal lonely dopamine rush, even if fleeting and artificial, is better than the relentless stress from cortisol.

Unlike anger, which is an approach emotion, contempt creates distance between you and the object of your contempt. With this distance between couples, reconciliatory action becomes less likely. You just don't want to be near your partner, let alone communicate with him or her. Communicating clearly for couples requires that they recognize and accept how intimately dependent on each other they are for the 3R's. When disrespect and contempt arise, they can create both anger and anxiety in the person who is the object of contempt. Imagine how that person now feels, recognizing that you do not see him or her as valuable, that you are withdrawing your 3R's, which includes protection, and leaving him or her vulnerable. The object of this contempt may become irrational in his or her effort to get you to change.

Families

Imagine that the story of Jane and Kevin were instead the story of a parent asking a teenager to take out the garbage, but not realizing that the kid is in the middle of a conversation with a friend or is doing homework or some other task. I see this all the time in my practice: a parent has a need to be met at a particular moment, but disregards that the child may be in the middle of something else. (This can also work the other way, in which a child makes a demand on a parent without recognizing that the parent is in the middle of something else. "I recognize you are hungry, but will feed you later," in whatever applicable form, is a worthwhile response for a parent to have at his or her disposal.) In many instances, a child's sense of time is not fully developed, whereas an adult already lives in a reality full of time pressures and deadlines. But a parent may feel disrespected if his child does not instantaneously execute his command. Compare the scenarios described here.

Poor communication. A father asks his son to take out the garbage, unaware that at that moment, his son is doing something else. The son appears to ignore him. Instead of stopping, looking, and listening, the father interprets the son's behavior as defying him, which evokes the father's suspicion, while the son interprets the father as being insensitive and commanding, evoking envy. The son ignores the father, who begins to shout in order to get the son to take out the garbage.

Anger response. The father's limbic system activates, and he becomes furious that his son does not give him the respect he feels he deserves, a foreshadowing of his losing value in the eyes of his child. As his anger mounts, his son's mirror neurons activate, and the son starts to believe that his father sees him as inadequate, without value, and therefore the subject of his father's rage. His own limbic system activates, and he feels a need either to defend himself or to leave the room, further escalating his father's anger.

Communicating clearly. The father stops, looks, and listens to see what his son is doing. He activates mirror neurons in his son, who stops, looks, and listens to his dad. The father sees that his son is involved in something else; he knows that taking out the garbage is an important responsibility but not urgent, so he asks his son if he wouldn't mind pausing in ten minutes to get the job done, then go back to his life. "If you need a reminder, I can do that too." The father has modeled respect of his son's time, a valuable resource, and asked for some of it to help the residence. In response, the son may say, "Sure, Dad, ten minutes would be great. I'll take care of it."

By using the Stop, Look, and Listen technique, the father has been able to assess what is happening with his son, and has influenced his son's response by starting with a foundation of projecting peace, engaging empathy, and then communicating clearly. In using the same technique, the son has assessed that his dad needs help, and negotiated a fair compromise with an anticipated result. These two primary PFC brains can share their resources, residence, and relationships by shifting away from the first three F's and fostering the fellowship of friendship. They are both reassuring each other of the value each brings to the family.

There's no getting around the realities of conflict in families, and many family members fight. When the fighting gets too pernicious and intractable, some of these families come to see someone like me, a psychiatrist. One simple technique I use in family therapy is to be sure that the members talk with each other directly, not through me. Rather than let a kid talk about her parent to me, I request that she turn her chair and tell her parent what she is thinking or feeling. Instead of everyone hearing, "My mom really bugs me," we all hear the kid say to the mom, "You really bug me." Being able to tolerate hearing this is a major part of beginning to communicate clearly. We have to be able to hear the negative in order to begin the transformation to the positive. We have to be able to recognize rage in order to engage empathy. If we do not stop, look, and listen, we shut down communicating clearly before it even has a chance.

Another technique is to find an area of agreement, even if it seems silly. For example, a kid may say that he and his father argue all the time. The father will often agree. I stop purposefully and ask them both to say what they said to each other instead of to me. The conversation may go like this: "Dad, we argue all the time." "Yeah, I've noticed," the father may respond. I then say with dramatized incredulity, "Wait a minute. Did the two of you just agree on something? That you argue all the time? When is the last time that happened? That you agreed?" The observation usually seems so silly to the two of them that they can both relax. A common ground has been found, even if they are simply agreeing that they have been arguing. From this common ground, the disrupted relationship can begin to be healed.

Bringing the communication to a mutual focus would not have happened if the father and son had kept talking to each other through me. It happened because they both stopped, looked, and listened to each other. You can do this at home during any argument, by simply acknowledging that you are arguing together. If you didn't matter to each other, you wouldn't care, and you might not even talk. Why waste the energy? It is in the disagreements and disappointments that we remind ourselves that what the other person thinks and feels about us *matters*. If we didn't care, we wouldn't want to be reassured that we are seen as valued. Most arguments are a desire to reestablish a certainty that we do indeed matter. We are angry because we do not think the other person sees us or our needs as valuable, and we want that to change.

The Workplace

Take the story of Kevin and Jane or of the boy and his dad, and now apply it to the workplace. A boss has asked her employee to get a report ready for tomorrow's meeting with the board. To prepare the report properly, the worker needs more information, but is too worried to ask. Will the boss think he is inadequate because he does not have the resources to get the job done, or will she provide him with what he needs so that he can give her what she needs?

Poor communication. The boss sends an email to the employee that she needs that report by tomorrow. Rather than disappoint her, he agrees right away, but does not deliver. Although he needed more information, he did not ask for it, and the boss is embarrassed the next day in front of her board. From her perspective, he has injured her and not treated her with respect. And from his, she has set him up for failure, regarding him as having no value and as expendable.

Anger response. Later that day, the boss storms into the employee's cubicle, calling him out in front of the rest of the office. Her anger prompts his mirror neurons to fire, and he gets defensive, saying that she assigned him an impossible task because she didn't give him all the information he needed to get the job done. She is now too limbic to be empathic and hears his words as an excuse. He realizes that she has power over him: the power to fire him and take all his resources, residence, and relationships, so he tries to flee, but this is seen by her as being even more disrespectful, and she fires him on the spot.

Communicating clearly. As soon as his boss asks for the report, the employee goes to her office and politely asks if she has the time to meet. She stops what she is doing, looks, and listens. He explains that he needs the additional information so that he won't let her down, sending a clear message that he knows how important this meeting is to her and the board. His message that he wants to seriously coop-erate activates her mirror neurons, and she is thus able to better engage empathy and communicate clearly just as he has done. She gives him the information he needs; her asking him to do the task and knowing she can rely on him both serve to recognize his value. From this platform of feeling respected and valued, as well as trusted, the employee produces a spectacular report, and his boss's value is elevated in the eyes of the board. The two have shared resources within their residence of work, and many, many relationships have been enhanced.

There is an added dividend to this kind of employee-employer rela-tionship. A boss who knows you have a loyalty and commitment to the job is also more likely to give you the time you need to attend to your family. Just as a partner who feels secure in the relationship sees you off to work confident about your commitment to him or her, so a boss who knows that you are committed to work can help you be more productive at home.

On a daily basis, anger can rise up at work, even if people share basically the same goal for the company. (Isn't it interesting that a workplace can be described as a company, the same word used to describe a collection of people hanging out together?) If not negoti-ated, such conflict can lead to disaster: loss of productivity, loss of revenue, even loss of your job. Whether one is in a jungle fending off predators or in a cubicle fending off a perceived competitor, the same biological mechanisms are at play.

By communicating clearly, everyone in these stories has become more successful. But to do this, each of them had to use Stop, Look, and

Listen. As always, this shift to the primary PFC yields remarkable dividends.

The Fourth F of Friendship Leads Away from Competition and Toward Cooperation

As the primary stress hormone, cortisol mobilizes our fight-flight mechanism in a way that emphasizes the survival of the individual, often at the expense of another individual. Unfortunately, the cortisol in one person impacts the production of cortisol in another person, and now you have two people in limbic survival mode. But when people cooperate instead of compete, cortisol levels are reduced. Spanish researchers compared cortisol levels in groups of women participating in a series of cooperative tasks. They showed that corti- sol levels were lower among the women who cooperated than among those who competed, suggesting that the modulator of that cortisol is positive cooperation. Cooperation entails communication, and communication with an aim of shared problem solving not only reduces cortisol but is likely to have been driven by enhanced oxyto- cin. By shifting from the limbic system to primary PFC, we can turn away from potential conflict. Instead, through PFC cooperation we can enhance the strength of our shared resources, residence, and relationships.

Have you ever worked with a teammate to get a job done? I used to do a lot of theater, and the pleasure of pulling together to get the show up and into production was unlike anything else. It is that spirit of friendship, trust, and cooperation that creates accomplishments and makes everyone in the group feel great: valued, respected, and successful. At home, work, or play, with a focus on resources, resi- dence, and relationships, what words can you use today to help another person feel valuable so that the two of you can get more done? And what words can you try to avoid using to prevent a limbic response? How can you contain someone else's anger, be empathic, try to understand the source, and then, like a Tai Chi expert, shift his or her anger flow into cooperative motion? No need to be confrontational or obstructive. Instead, you can take that angry energy and guide it to your advantage. You have the first six steps already.

ON A SOCIETAL LEVEL

As you know quite well by now, anger stems from a perceived threat to resources, residence, or relationships. But where do values, be they moral or ethical, fit into this schema? One could consider a value a shared resource between people in relationships who are living and occupying the same residence. The same view can be applied to religious beliefs, cultural practices, or political ideologies. With this view, we can see how conflict over these personal, community, and even national values could lead to anger.

Negotiation is the art of getting to a satisfactory agreement between parties. By definition, it is the action of resolving disagreements or the navigation of a hazard or problem. Negotiators often will concede when confronting anger, a gesture of respect that begins to calm the other party's brain. Concession does not mean giving up but rather being able to work toward a middle ground. Negotiators are willing to offer compromises when negotiating about things and interests. In fact, some advantage may have been biological and evolutionarily promoted if an angry person can get a competitor to negotiate and perhaps back down, at least over resources.

But Dutch researchers have suggested recently in the *British Journal of Social Psychology* that this same strategy of using anger backfires if the conflict is over values. When that happens, even a negotiator is more likely not to back down, instead retaliating, escalating the disagreement, and getting angry himself. People have different views and perspectives, but these run the risk of pushing us into in-groups and out-groups. Finding common ground is always possible, even if that commonality is as abstract as sharing a desire for justice and fairness. Even if we disagree about what constitutes fairness, we both still want the same thing. The process of how we get to these agreements is under active investigation.

A 2010 *Harvard Business Review* article outlined successful negotiation strategies, and all of them seem like PFC functions. When implemented, these basic principles are used to "resolve conflict and influence others: maintaining a big-picture perspective; uncovering hidden agendas to improve collaboration; using facts and fairness to get buy-in; building trust; and focusing on process as well as outcomes."

COMMUNICATION AND HUMAN PROGRESS

Even though not all of us are partners, parents, CEOs, or diplomats, we make important decisions that have an influence on other people all the time. Each of us has legitimate needs and wants. Each of us has a drive to survive and a need to be valued. When you look at these basic individual needs, the potential for anger is enormous if we think we cannot meet our needs except at the expense of others or if another person's anger might derail our objectives. The struggle over the control of resources has been the legacy of much of human history. Communication, powerful as it can be, has sometimes been exploited.

For instance, charismatic influence in the form of religious leadership has been shown to take what seems to be clear communication and actually short-circuit logical, PFC abilities. In a noteworthy Danish study published in 2011, fMRIs of religious participants showed dramatic shifts in their blood-oxygen-level-dependent (BOLD) responses, an indicator that parts of their brains were more activated than others, in response to a charismatic speaker who they believed had healing abilities. In their wish to believe, these religious followers actually *de*activated their PFC, suggesting that they had abandoned the logical part of their brain and were responding in a more limbic, emotionally driven fervor. One can only hope that the influence of these leaders over their flocks is being used for positive endeavors, as of course has not always been the case.

Language is extremely powerful and can be misused by casting suspicion and envy on those perceived as being outside an in-group. A chilling exhibit at the Holocaust Museum in Washington DC explores how a decade of Nazi propaganda—communications designed to distract and obfuscate—produced a powerful lack of empathy toward an identified out-group. The propaganda was designed to engender indifference toward those people whose homes and businesses were being confiscated and who were herded onto overcrowded trains and shipped away. This indifference is also a function of communication, and the dangers of the human ability to deceive must not be lightly regarded or overlooked.

Unfortunately, there is still much racism and bigotry in the world, and those who see other people with contempt and disgust are pretty good at communicating that clearly. These attitudes never go unnoticed and more often than not create the same reaction in the so-called out-group. This was exactly the finding published by researchers at the University of St. Andrews in Scotland recently. Muslims surveyed in India and Britain who felt that they were being unfairly discriminated against created an in-group fellowship more likely to react with irrational responses. They returned perceived contempt with contempt, and were less likely to try to engage in any negotiation, as contempt leads to distancing and minimal desire for reconciliation.

Global politics are mirrored in local politics every day. Take office politics, for example. What happens when you have a coworker you don't like, and you make no effort to hide it? Usually nothing good. But rather than be phony and untrue about your feelings, try stepping back, using the first three steps in outsmarting anger, and recognizing that your contempt is another manifestation of anger. What don't you like about that person? Is he doing something annoying because he knows it bugs you or because he is oblivious to the fact that it bugs you? If the latter, he may have unwittingly activated your flight-fight mechanism: if he doesn't care about you and has no empathy, then you perceive him as a danger. And if he is doing something purposefully to tick you off, rather than go limbic yourself and escalate, use the first three steps: recognize, categorize, and rate your anger. If your anger is based on envy or suspicion, move your brain from limbic to primary PFC mode. You have every right to let a person know he is bugging you. But how you let him know will either result in continued conflict or create cooperation.

What conflicts have you faced today with a partner, parent, child, or coworker? With a teacher or even the person preparing your coffee at the local store? Have you been able to see her big picture, her hidden agenda? Have you treated her fairly and with respect, and planned how to get things done together so that you can both be more successful? Remember, every exchange between two people has the potential to go in a number of ways, just as it did for the tired couple at the beginning of this chapter, who had the opportunity either to have an angry fight or to outsmart their anger and embrace peace for the good of the whole family.

Communicating clearly is a strategy that is applicable between in-groups and out-groups as small as two different people or as large as nations, ethnic groups, or religions. When you use your PFC to communicate clearly, you have the opportunity to activate that fourth alternative: friendship. The first step in this endeavor can be as simple as saying thank you.

Trade Thanks

God gave you a gift of 86,400 seconds today.
Have you used one to say "thank you"?
—William A. Ward (1921–1994)

Silent gratitude isn't much use to anyone.
—G. B. Stern (1890–1973)

Recently I went back to New York City to see some Broadway shows. I always stay across from the site of the World Trade Center towers, and always feel a little sad and bewildered at the gravity of what occurred. There amid the life and movement of the city rest the two large, ever-flowing pools that memorialize the people lost, even as the two new buildings grow steadily toward the heavens, constructed by the people who remain. Sheathed in mirrored glass, they reflect the tenacity and declaration of what human beings truly are: survivors who have learned to endure in concert with each other.

I waited for my turn in line at the Will Call box office for my tickets that I had bought months in advance—six tickets for myself, my wife, two of my kids who were with us, and my elderly cousins. The ticket guy looked for my tickets, then returned with a serious look on his face: there were no tickets in my name for tonight. Somehow the ticket agency had booked us for the following Tuesday, and this was Saturday. I felt my cortisol level rising. The ticket booth guy went on to apologize for the mix-up with the tickets, but assured me he would put things right.

From behind me came a burly, irritated voice of a large New Yorker. He leaned over my shoulder and snapped at the ticket guy, saying he wanted his tickets and asking what was taking so long. The ticket guy politely told the man that there was a problem with another customer (me) and that he was trying to solve it. The man did not take this kindly, instead snarling and growling his discontent and saying that if the ticket guy had known it was going to take so long, he should have served him first.

I found myself saying out loud, "This fellow is solving my problem. When he is done, I have no doubt he is skilled enough to then address yours." The man huffed some more and said it was a shoddy arrangement and pushed himself to the front of the line to my right. I caught my first glimpse of him: a large salt-and-pepper-haired man, standing a good six feet five.

My ticket guy looked apologetically at me, but said he had found six house seats for the show: four in the second row and two in the row directly behind. He was sorry that we were not going to be seated together, but it was the best he could do. I was delighted that he had found a solution, and gave him my heartfelt thanks. He smiled. My cortisol level decreased, and so did his. What could have erupted in anger and disappointment was transformed into a shared moment of triumph.

I looked over at the angry man. He had cut in line, intimidating the people behind him with his clear display of anger. He grabbed at the tickets handed to him by the ticket person, reiterated his irritation, and stormed away without a thank you. He did not notice the people in his line glare at him for cheating, nor the look of relief on the face of the ticket person who had helped him. I shrugged in acknowledgment of the angry fellow as I looked again at the person who had found great seats for me, thanked him once more, and accepted his smile and sincere "You're welcome. Enjoy the show."

We went into the theater and headed down the aisle toward the front. A small commotion was occurring as we entered, and there, in the very last row of the theater, the angry man was fighting to get to his seat, accompanied by a young woman with crutches struggling to get by the knees and feet of the seated audience. Even as the angry man made the people already situated get up so that the two could muscle by, he said not a word of thanks. The ones he passed sat down annoyed, and the ones ahead seemed to rise with enormous reluctance and in no haste. The angry man found his seat, but before he sat, he turned to help the girl, took her crutches, and with a gentleness I did not expect, held her elbow as she labored to balance and ease herself into her chair.

The first act went so fast, was so delightful, that I was astonished when it was already time for intermission. With a throng of audience members, I made my way to the restrooms. There, waiting outside the bathroom, was the salt-and-pepper-haired fellow. Our eyes met. I walked over to him even as he bristled.

"Sorry about the confusion up there," I started. My apology caught him by surprise. His entire demeanor softened, and he replied, "It wasn't your fault." I explained to him the problem I had faced, and he then explained his. The young woman he was with was his daughter, who had a significant disability. He noticed her beginning to wilt as they waited for their tickets, standing with difficulty for a prolonged amount of time. He began to feel angry, wanting to protect his daughter. He just needed someone to help him get his tickets so that he and his child could go and sit down in the theater.

In the blink of an eye, we judge each other. In the blink of an eye, our limbic brain activates our survival mode. But with the blink of an eye, we can reengage our PFC, recognize our instincts, and then outsmart them with our intellect.

I remarked how I understood that all he wanted to do was protect his kid. Then I put out my hand and told him that my name was Joe. He extended his hand and told me his name. And we shook. I thanked him for telling me his story, and hoped he was enjoying the show. "You're welcome," he replied. "Thanks for asking. Thanks for coming over." For the rest of the evening, whenever we saw each other, we would smile, wave, and call each other by name. We built a tower of understanding and, I believe, a mutual respect.

If I had not gone over to chat with him, had I turned away in anger and disgust, I would never have found out why he had been so urgently trying to get his tickets. I would have, instead, perhaps lumped him as yet another uncouth pushy person, selfishly trying to get his way over the needs of others. And I would have been wrong, and would have wronged a father who was just trying to prevent his child with a disability from falling down. Like a twin tower.

I started this book with another New York story, one in which I was intimidated and angered by an angry man. He may never read this book, but I actually want to thank him. He got me wondering about this anger thing, why it happens, and how we can outsmart this most dangerous of our emotions. Other chapters of this book have provided the first six strategies for doing so, all of which pave and promote the neural pathways for our PFC to take charge. This final strategy will seem remarkably familiar and simple to you. We have an opportunity to outsmart anger in each other every day, and most of us do it intuitively and instinctively: we *trade thanks.*

When we trade thanks, we acknowledge the positive contribution someone has made to our lives. Whether to the man at the ticket booth, the lady at the coffee shop, the stranger who holds open the elevator door, or the person with whom you decide to spend the rest of your life, the simple act of gratitude, of saying thank you, has a positive impact on that individual's brain. And it's not unilateral. When the other person says "You're welcome" in response, it is a signal that the boundaries have been lowered and you are "welcome" into his or her group. You are not seen with envy or suspicion, but have been deemed safe enough to be given access to the other person's life, to his resources. "You're welcome" implies an entry into her residence and that she has included you as part of her in-group. A conversation may ensue, and from there, a possible relationship between individuals, a possibility of the fellowship of friendship.

Thus, trading thanks is one of the most powerful ways you can influence the level of anger in people surrounding you. You have learned how to project peace, engage empathy, and communicate clearly. Trading thanks serves to naturally, proactively extend your capability to outsmart another's innate and dangerous emotion. Your brain influences the brains of others, either readying them for an altruistic act in the future or a retaliatory one. In most situations, you have the power to choose to make a foe or a friend.

SMALL THANKS ARE A BIG DEAL

All parents teach their children to say thank you, yet people don't often think about the reasons why. What does this "polite" act really accomplish? In a human exchange, the simple gratitude conveyed by a thank you shows basic respect to the giver. When you show respect to someone, you are conveying that you value her. Think about when someone refuses to trade thanks. He is universally thought to be rude because he has upset the natural social order. We often react by becoming angry and suspicious, even contemptuous. "I let the guy ahead of me, and he didn't even say thanks!"

Parents may experience this with some frequency. They have been paying for resources and residence in the spirit of the relationship, but their kid may still respond with a grunt and a sense of irritation when asked to empty the dishwasher or take out the garbage. This sense of ingratitude can really get under a parent's skin, having an immediate impact on his or her cortisol level; and as quickly as a match ignites dry kindling, a parent's brain can get angry. But why do we react this way? If anger is an emotion designed to change the behavior of others, what is it we want when we feel a lack of gratitude? What is it we want to change when we feel exploited?

Once again, it comes down to the basic desire of all of us to simply feel valued by another human being. Be it our spouse or partner, our kids, our boss, the people we serve as a waitress, or the driver we have just let into our lane of traffic, we want and need to be acknowledged as a valuable resource, residence, or relationship to someone else. We want to assure our safe place in the group so that we need not fear having to fend for ourselves.

Saying thank you switches from red to green the "person approval" light in someone else's brain. On a biological level, this positive social interaction triggers the release of neurochemicals, such as oxytocin, inspiring a mutually positive feeling between the participants of the exchange. This is a difference in perception that happens in just milliseconds. One moment you are a stranger or possible threat, the next a respectful and respected citizen and possibly a person with whom someone could engage. You have shifted a brain from being mistrusting to holding the potential for trust. When two parties exchange a "thank you" and a "you're welcome," they make a significant connection. By trading thanks, you are expressing gratitude. You have expanded your options from flight-fight-freeze to friendship and the cooperative advantage implied by that relationship.

Gratitude as a concept is quite ancient. A highly praised human attribute found in religious teachings from Islam to Judaism, from Christianity to Buddhism, it has been considered an emotion, an idea, a virtue, or a prism through which to view one's life. The word itself stems from the Latin *gratia*, which basically translates as "grace." But *gratia* is also the root of other words like *grateful* and *gracious*, words that connote kindness, giving, and unconditional love. *Dei gratia*, for instance, means "by the grace of god" in Latin. But only recently have psychology and neuroscience researchers studied the experience and practice of gratitude.

Numerous surveys and experiments, especially within the positive psychology movement of the last decade, have been showing how gratitude leads to well-being on a great many levels. Recently, psychologists Robert Emmons and Michael McCullough, with their team at UC Davis, have focused intensely on the benefits of gratitude and published numerous studies showing its impact on life fulfillment and health. One way they have been able to measure gratitude is by having volunteers keep "gratitude journals." By analyzing the participants and their recordings over time, the researchers have been able to show that those who feel more grateful have higher levels of life satisfaction, vitality, and positive emotions. This group rates as more generous, more empathic, more helpful, and less envious of others. They are also more likely to acknowledge "a belief in the interconnectedness of all life and a commitment to and responsibility to others."

But there is a difference between being grateful for what you have and showing another person gratitude for what he or she has given. The first is the proverbial "count your blessings." The second is to recognize the blessing of another person's behaviors toward you. It is in this outward expression of gratitude that we have an enormous and positive influence on another person's brain.

Grateful thinking and the expression of gratitude appear to have a huge impact in many areas of human interaction, especially in creating relationships. Indeed, the more you trade thanks and show gratitude, the better your chances of building and maintaining relationships. A recent University of North Carolina study published in the journal *Emotion* examined the role of naturally occurring gratitude among a group where it was vitally important to build new relationships—a college sorority. Each year at the University of Virginia, sororities hold Big Sister Week, a special time when new sorority members, Little Sisters, are pampered anonymously by a Big Sister. Big Sister Week is viewed as a way to welcome new members into the sorority group. The Big Sisters give gifts and plan events for their Little Sisters, then reveal their identities at the end of the week. For the study, the Little Sisters completed an online questionnaire after they received something from a Big Sister. They briefly described the event and also answered questions about their feelings. Both the Big and Little Sisters also answered questions about the quality of their new relationship at the end of the week and a month later.

When the researchers looked at the results of the surveys, they found two things. The first was that the more benefits the Little Sisters received, the more they reported feeling gratitude. Perhaps there is no surprise there. When given a resource, most people are appreciative, as it has enhanced their well-being. But the second finding was much more interesting. Big Sisters who felt more appreciated by Little Sisters went on to have closer and more rewarding relationships with their new sorority members. When their efforts were recognized and they were given thanks, a stronger bond was created between the benefactor and the recipient. This is very important, revealing the power of trading thanks. One can imagine what the Big Sisters who did not get such thanks experienced: probably feelings approaching anger and disgust for their Little Sister.

When you give something, large or small, to someone who doesn't express thanks, how does it make you feel about that person? Angry? Disgusted? Contemptuous? Exploited? You may perceive her as a "taker"—of resources, residence, or relationships. She has cheated and capitalized on your altruism without giving anything back to make you feel good about what you did. Although most of us are charitable without consciously desiring accolades and acknowledgment, think about this in your own experience. If you volunteer to do a job and do not get thanked, chances are you will be less likely to volunteer again. As a result of not receiving gratitude, you may be less inclined to share with the person and also less likely to place trust in the relationship.

The opposite occurs when people express gratitude consistently and, in particular, when they do so verbally. When you get praised and thanked for helping out, you feel valued and acknowledged. Recently my wife read a story to a first-grade class. The teacher had the kids make a huge card of thanks and give it to my wife. She was beaming, and is now determined to read for those kids again. This is a smart teacher. By having her students make and send that card, she both expressed gratitude to my wife and taught her students a valuable lesson: when someone gives of her time, be sure to acknowledge the gift.

A woman who was getting a divorce felt angry and bitter at her ex, talking about him in a therapy session. It was not so much that he did not love her anymore but that he showed no gratitude for all she had done in their marriage: moving from one part of the country to another to help his career, being available and supportive, helping raise the kids, doing the little things that showed him his value.

Another patient had suffered a freak accident, leaving him fighting to regain the use of his legs. He was understandably angry at God for his crippling injury, but felt secure that his wife was there to help him through it. Unfortunately, he never told her, even though he was incredibly grateful that she did not leave him and stayed in their marriage. He never told her how much she meant to him, but would stew in his anger. He only spoke to her about his rage, but never about how grateful he was for her being there to bear witness and love him.

Not telling her was a huge mistake. His wife began to feel more and more exploited and not appreciated for staying to care for him. Eventually she could not tolerate his rage and became rageful herself, resenting that his focus was on all he had lost and not on her being still there to help him. Their marriage began to stagnate. But she did not tell him that she felt as trapped and paralyzed by his apparent lack of appreciation as she supposed he felt by his injury. Instead, she asked for a divorce, which enraged him even more. He felt she was abandoning him, attributing her intention to the lost use of his legs, the resultant lost income for the family, and her seeing him as inadequate and useless. Not until he was able to overcome his anger toward her and let her know in therapy how much she meant to him, to thank her for all she had done, was she able to feel some relief and rekindle the love and attachment between them.

The more you express gratitude, the more the recipient of this gratitude experiences what psychologists call the "communal strength" of a relationship. Expressing gratitude can thus be a powerful way to harvest the resources of another, for someone who feels a high degree of communal strength is more motivated to respond to the needs of the other person in the relationship. In a recent study, researchers at the University of Florida asked one group to express gratitude to a friend, while another group was asked to think grateful thoughts or have positive interactions with a friend. The perceived communal strength was highest among the people to whom gratitude was expressed. But, according to this study, the *thinking* gratitude was not found to be good enough. You have to *communicate* it clearly and not just rely on someone's mirror neurons and empathy. The real message here is to be sure not to take someone for granted: let him know how valuable he really is by telling him out loud.

GRATITUDE'S GIFT

American philosopher and psychology pioneer William James was spot-on when he wrote, "The deepest principle in human nature is the craving to be appreciated." When we ask ourselves why trading thanks matters, and why it works, James's wise observation still holds true. With these words, he echoes the main idea we've been exploring in this book. When you behave in a certain way toward other people, tapping in to what you know about how the human brain is designed, you have the ability to influence other people's emotions, especially their anger. Trading thanks, as simple as it sounds, meets the fundamental need of all people to feel appreciated and valued, reducing their potential for anger.

Modern psychological science is delving into the specific details of *how* gratitude works to bond humans together. Researchers at the Wharton School in Pennsylvania, for example, examined how an expression of gratitude motivated certain people to be more helpful. In a series of experiments, the first set asking participants to help a student write a job application cover letter, and the other to respond to a university fundraiser, they looked at the differences in responses and why participants either helped further or stopped helping in both gratitude-receiving and non-gratitude-receiving situations.

In examining the results, the researchers explored two potential reasons for continued helpful, prosocial behavior: self-efficacy and social worth. When self-efficacy is the motivating factor, a person's sense of value in herself is increased internally. The helping makes her feel competent and proud of herself. But when social worth motivates a person to continue helping, it implies a perception that another person valued him, an external influence. Both self-efficacy and social worth can act as motivators to help. But when it came to helping someone again, the data told a clear and compelling story: in the letter-writing experiments, a mere expression of thanks more than doubled the likelihood that helpers would provide assistance again. In the fundraising experiments, gratitude produced more than 50 percent increases in the number of calls that the average fundraiser made in a single week. The expression of gratitude had a powerful effect in motivating people to be helpful because it enabled them to feel socially valued. When you feel valuable in the eyes of another person, you can unleash your human potential. Being respected leads to feeling valued, and being valued leads to trust.

But when you are not thanked, you can begin to lose trust in that person, feeling less and less valued and more and more resentful and angry. You want that person to change and to let you know that he will indeed be there for you sometime in the future if you need him. A person who feels socially valued feels safer. She is recognized as a contributing member of the in-group and has a lower risk of being thrown out of the group and, in ancient times, perhaps becoming a predator's lunch. The act of trading thanks, of acknowledging value, can also create a promise for future altruism, of binding ourselves to each other to expand and fortify our in-groups. Our mutual gratitude today is a promise of mutual help tomorrow. Your ingratitude today can breed anger and resentment, threatening to deprive you of access to resources, residence, and relationships, and to the safety of a larger group.

THE BENEFACTOR-BENEFICIARY BOND

It is in this promise of future altruism that the bonding of giver and receiver can take hold. Indeed, scientists consider gratitude as a way to induce social affiliation, or create an in-group. This makes survival sense: a person wants to remain close to another person from whom

WARY MEN, WELCOME WOMEN

We know that being valued makes people feel good, but some things make people feel better than others—value has variability. It turns out that what gives women a sense of being valued can be quite different than what helps men feel valued. Those were the findings from researchers at George Mason University in Virginia, whose recent study showed that women had an easier time expressing gratitude than men and felt less burden and obligation when receiving a gift. Also, those women who showed more gratitude felt more connected to a group, which then led them to feel more capable and autonomous.

But for men the results were very different. Men had a harder time receiving gifts, especially if they were older and the benefactor was another man. The men thought that expressing gratitude was not a simple thing at all and even three months later felt more burdened and less independent. The implications of this finding are disturbing. In a world where men have expected to be dominant, where getting a gift or expressing thanks can be seen as a weakness, men are at much higher risk of succumbing to the limbic responses of envy or suspicion. Perhaps this tendency stems from the social idea that men are meant to be providers, and being given a gift implies that they have limited resources. This limbic view of who we are is a clear path to anger, envy, or suspicion. But even men have evolved a PFC. Rather than interpret gratitude as a covert implication of weakness, men can see gratitude as a way to bring their band of hunters closer together, appreciating that there is no "I" in team. Humans are not individual runners in a marathon. We are a relay team trying to help each other across a global finish line where we can all be more successful, each awarded with a first-place medal.

he receives benefit. But how exactly does the benefactor make out in this deal? Why would she want to remain connected to those on the receiving end? In fact, it is quite amazing that acts of altruism do not activate anger. After all, if I am doing something for you, it may imply I have more power—more resources, residence, or relationships. Why would this not activate envy in you and then suspicion in me?

Psychologists at Gonzaga University in Washington State looked into this question in a 2012 study, published in *Cognition & Emotion*, and found that a beneficiary will to do things for a benefactor, even at a cost to himself. When a benefactor extends her mantle of power, giving of her resources, it creates a relationship in which the beneficiary is then willing to go that extra mile on the benefactor's behalf and does not become envious. This may explain why volunteers make phone calls or canvas a neighborhood for their political candidate, or why an employee may be loyal and faithful to his boss, even if it means staying late at the office.

But the Gonzaga team found something else in the same study: the receipt of gratitude motivates continued beneficence. When a person experiences being thanked—an acknowledgment of her beneficence—it feels good. To get that good feeling again, a benefactor may just remain nearby to be available the next time her beneficence is required. It is the expression of gratitude for what one has received that serves to bind a benefactor to the beneficiary. This gratitude decreases the possibility that the benefactor will become suspicious that the beneficiary will try to take more resources than are being offered. The reciprocity between benefactor and beneficiary has expanded the group: a clear survival advantage for both.

But gratitude can strike an even deeper chord among people. It can become contagious. Many studies have shown a "spillover" effect in human generosity when people experience grateful feelings. Many people have heard of the term "pay it forward"—to bestow a kindness upon a total stranger with no expectation of a return favor or even a thanks. I give to you, a total stranger, with the intention that you give on to the next. What these observations suggest to scientists is that gratitude—and a grateful framework—may encourage prosocial behaviors that promote cooperation. With increased cooperation, groups can enhance their ability to survive and thrive—a key reason why the experience and practice of gratitude have evolved in humans and can be found throughout virtually all ethnic groups in the world.

Exercise: Self-Help That Helps Others

When you trade thanks, you are not exclusively helping others but also helping yourself. Try this the next time you are in a drive-through at a coffee shop: when the barista takes your order, offer to pay for the person either in front of or behind you. I do this on a regular basis, especially when I see a police car either in front of or behind me. Police officers do so much for us, and often with so little acknowledgment. Usually the person in front turns around with a huge grin of astonishment and appreciation. You may never know what the person in back of you may do, but my guess is that she will feel the same way. Perhaps she will get the idea to pay for a stranger's coffee next time. A few days ago, I was at the drive-through service counter of a local coffee place. The barista told me that the customer in the car behind me had paid for my coffee! I stuck my head out the window, craned my neck, and waved my thanks. He waved back, also smiling. "You did it for me about six months ago!" the man shouted. "Thanks," I shouted back, and drove away smiling and delighted.

Gratitude has even been shown to impact economic relationships. For a long time, economists believed that a human being was motivated selfishly to get more stuff at the expense of someone else. This cynical view made sense if you adopted a dog-eat-dog view of evolution, in which survival of the fittest was typified by Alfred, Lord Tennyson's phrase "nature red in tooth and claw." But our understanding of how humans work together has grown significantly since Darwin.

There is ample evidence showing that gratitude can modulate self-interest, shifting a person from seeking only individual financial gain to pursuing an interest in communal profit. Northeastern University researchers, for instance, have shown that giving is not confined just to someone you know personally. In a money game experiment, participants who were thanked for their financial donation were 25 percent more likely to donate again for the communal good, even if it decreased their personal wealth. Even more encouraging, the increased giving occurred whether the beneficiary was known or a complete stranger. This intriguing effect suggests that the generosity of a human being is not limited, as has been previously believed, to a person from whom you expect to get something back at a future date.

Of course, a cynical interpretation of this thinking takes us back to the topic of envy: giving through charity becomes a way to preempt another person from wanting what you have and taking it by force. We may be wired to give to complete strangers, but it's with a self-serving motivation to avoid conflict. But a more hopeful view is to wonder if we are becoming aware that the larger the in-group, the more that other people have, the better off we all will be. Granted, this may ultimately still be self-serving, but with a different motivation. Rather than giving to ward off an attack, we give because we feel good ourselves, especially when we are clearly acknowledged for our contribution. Humans do indeed seem to break the animal mold of only showing altruism or sharing resources, residence, or relationships with their relatives.

Although this is a finding with dramatic implications for charity, civic duty, and other forms of social good, it is equally important for a kindergarten child who learns to share his crayons or to thank a guest reader (who is then thanked in return by the teacher and beneficiary). Or for the boss who thanks her workers for doing such a great job. Or for a worker who thanks his boss for assiduously enforcing a workplace safety policy. Or for a kid who takes out the garbage, or a spouse who buys the milk. And if you are on the receiving end of a benefit, expressing your gratitude seems to make the benefactor want to keep helping. These types of behaviors, amazingly simple in themselves, bring people together and push anger, suspicion, and envy to the sidelines.

TAKE NOTHING FOR GRANTED

Saying thank you is so easy and so simple. We can all do it and benefit from both saying thanks and being the recipient of thanks. In fact, trading thanks is a very good trade with really excellent returns. So how can we consistently integrate trading thanks into our homes, workplace, and community? The simple answer is to start simply. Use your PFC to identify another person's strengths, and let him or her know that you appreciate them. Thank people for their contribution and see what happens.

Family and Close Friends

Sometimes the very people who are closest to us and most important in our lives are those to whom we express the least gratitude. Our daily routines tend to get in the way. Parents are often experiencing high levels of stress as they juggle multiple responsibilities and perhaps struggle to make ends meet. Children too get busy with homework, sports, and social activities and don't think about what trading thanks means. If not taught otherwise, kids will go through life without understanding the value of writing a thank-you note or email to a grandparent for a birthday gift. Why then would you expect this same child to learn to trade thanks at school or work in their future lives? It's critically important for parents and other adults to slow down and model trading thanks to children so that it becomes a habit, yes, but a conscious one. It will affect all their other relationships throughout life.

Children and teens can be at high risk for not feeling valued, especially if they are struggling in academics or experiencing social challenges. They are particularly vulnerable when hearing messages of failure, of not making enough effort, of being a source of stress to a parent or teacher. In terms of early brain and emotional development, these messages are exactly the opposite of what kids need to be hearing regularly. As you'll recall, the third choice in the fight-flight response is to freeze. In freeze mode, people try to become as still as possible, invisible, overwhelmed by the impending danger. Not fast enough to flee or strong enough to fight, they freeze and hope the danger passes, shivering in fear. This is not just avoidance but feeling powerless. I believe that in the human experience, the freeze response translates into depression, a profound inertia in which everything slows down and one loses a sense of purpose and ability. I see this freeze phenomenon among many of the kids I treat, but also see how this emotional inertia can kindle, ignite, and explode into anger. Sometimes this anger is turned against the person himself or herself, and self-harm in the form of drug abuse and suicide attempts can ensue.

But parents can influence and counteract feelings of low worth in many small but significant ways, and trading thanks is one of them. Simply showing a child that you are truly grateful that she is sharing your resources, residence, and relationships communicates your appreciation and respect. A child who feels respected feels valued. A child who sees herself as valuable through your eyes learns to trust. A child who trusts can unleash her unlimited human potential. The child with potential is not a powerless child. With the support of others, with the acknowledgment of value, a child—a person of any age—need not feel powerless and overwhelmed.

In fact, Chinese psychologists recently showed that gratitude has a protective effect on the lives of students. In their 2012 study published in the *Journal of Adolescence*, students who experienced gratitude from others reported higher self-esteem and lower incidence of suicidal thoughts and suicide attempts. When you feel that someone else sees you as valuable, and expresses this by thanking you, why would you feel less valuable or want to harm yourself? It feels great to be acknowledged.

In another study focused on students, University of South Carolina researchers showed that experiencing gratitude contributed to a sense of well-being, and was a major component in helping a student feel successful academically and socially. Other helpful factors included personal goal setting, structured mentoring or life coaching, problem solving, and having good interpersonal skills. If you think about it, these are mostly PFC functions that involve planning, anticipation, and social connection.

Couples and spouses also fare better when using their PFC, and trading thanks is something that brings couples together and builds a strong and lasting foundation. When couples express gratitude toward each other, they are showing how much they value one another and are willing to put energy into the upkeep of the relationship. When couples take each other for granted, it can be the first step down a lonely road. But by regularly expressing gratitude, couples are effectively keeping open the door of communication. Researchers from the Family Institute at Florida State University discovered that couples who more easily expressed gratitude were also more able to talk about concerns in the relationship. When you have a foundation of trust and appreciation, it feels safer to let the other person know your worries. How different this is than holding on to hidden hurts that can fester, only to further erode the relationship. If gratitude can help keep the door open, it's worth a try.

But once in the door, it really comes down to letting your partner know that he or she is amazing and appreciated: this is achieved by trading thanks. It comes as no surprise that couples who do not keep up positive communication are more likely to get divorced. But even those couples who were happily married as newlyweds can be vulnerable to conflict if they don't positively reinforce one another, according to a 2012 UCLA study published in the *Journal of Family Psychology*. Psychologists studied 136 couples who identified themselves as very happy and satisfied during the first four years of their marriage. They then compared the couples who stayed married with those who went on to divorce by the tenth year. The common factor among the divorced couples was a higher rate of negative communication during the new-lywed years. It may go without saying that negative communication rarely includes expressions of gratitude and appreciation, but rather those of blame, disgust, and contempt.

Workplace and Community

Every day, we go to work and interact with colleagues, managers, clients, the public, and others. In each of these relationships, we have the opportunity to trade thanks or not, but when we do, we enhance other people's well-being and our own at the place where most of us spend the better part of our days. Gratitude becomes a resource we can wield in our work residence to enhance relationships with our colleagues. Don't we all feel most productive and rewarded in a work-place where we feel appreciated by colleagues, supervisors, and cus-tomers? This appreciation can be expressed in the form of direct praise, thanks, and sometimes a bonus or pay raise. It makes sense that if you feel appreciated at work and feel gratitude toward your employer, you are less likely to look for a different job, and may put in extra time without complaining.

In fact, a sense of gratitude toward an employer has even been shown to mediate disappointment when employees' pay gets cut. A 2012 study by researchers at the University of Auckland and UCLA found that of 953 university faculty members who had received invol-untary pay reductions, those who felt gratitude responded differently in terms of their level of disappointment than those who felt anger, fear, or sadness. They were much more likely to express loyalty to the university, despite the pay cut. If a work culture with an administra-tion that appreciates its employees can help prevent sour grapes when salaries gets cut, then such a culture could undoubtedly pay off in the long run in terms of loyalty and productivity.

We've all heard about the alternative: the company where there's high turnover and people complain chronically, even when the pay is good. One of the reasons for this may be that workers don't feel that employers are giving them adequate appreciation or respect for their efforts. Perhaps employees seek more acknowledgment than just a paycheck for working hard and taking a job seriously. A culture of disrespect can increase stress levels and even wear down workers' morale. Canadian researchers looked into this dynamic in a field that's frequently rife with disrespect: restaurant service. Their study, looking at the impact of entitled customers' behavior on waitstaff, illustrated how damaging such disrespect can be. Waitstaff reported feelings of burnout, of their bodies responding negatively, and, more ominously, of being dehumanized. Often they felt alone and abandoned by their managers when they were provided minimal workplace support. When employees are laboring under such stressful conditions and lacking support from colleagues and management, it's no surprise that a restaurant, or any company for that matter, would struggle to retain workers.

Another result of a low-appreciation, low-gratitude workplace is the tendency for workers to stop caring, avoid responsibility, and assign blame. We have all experienced this feeling to a degree. Your heart isn't in a particular project or task, and you decide not to take ownership of it; when something goes wrong, what do you do? Point the finger. But the main problem with blaming others is that you are actually abdicating responsibility. And if it is always someone else's fault, you are never in control. If you are never in control, you will always be anxious, living in a limbic, cortisol-driven fight-flight-freeze modality. When your brain is in limbic mode, you are more likely to get angry, desperately trying to change someone else's behavior that seems to threaten your 3R's. Blaming other people keeps you limbic and not in PFC mode. And because the other person sees you blaming him, he in turn becomes defensive, activating his own anger response to get you to change your behavior and stop blaming him. Being blamed implies he has done something wrong, has lost value, and doesn't deserve respect.

On a broader community level, blame can take on an even more insidious quality, as demonstrated in a 2011 study by researchers at the

University of Queensland, in which blame was found to serve as a means of dehumanizing an out-group, allowing the in-group to perform all sorts of atrocities. Similar to the waitstaff person who was trapped in the position of serving an entitled customer, someone who is continually blamed begins to see herself through the eyes of others as worthless. This is the dark side of ToM at work, overriding an individual's own sense of value. When we blame someone else, we have the unfortunate ability to then view him or her as lacking in moral value, and not as equally human as ourselves. If another person is "less human," then we think we can abdicate our moral responsibility and connection to him or her, and disengage empathy rather than engage it.

This kind of moral abandonment plagues human history, as societies have needlessly and recklessly exercised blame in the form of scapegoating. Racism, bigotry, sexism, religious persecution, and genocides have at their core a terrifying human ability to dehumanize another, justifying aggression and the forcible removal or denial of the 3R's. But if one person is capable of this antisocial and dangerous behavior, everyone else has the same capacity. Do any of us want to be on the other side of such a blaming in-group? Blame serves to perpetuate the mythology of a noble in-group and a devious out-group of subhumans. It is only a matter of which side you take that relegates you to the other group. In small ways, we all have experienced being part of an out-group, either by being bullied at school or at work or by being the focus of prejudice on a larger scale. And in many other ways, we live in a blame culture. Sometimes it feels as though nobody wants to take responsibility. Who's to blame for our failing schools? Who's to blame for childhood obesity? Who's to blame for the economy, high fuel prices, and greenhouse gases? This list goes on, but the blame can stop if we individually and then collectively take on the responsibility and work together to solve these social problems. Evolution has produced an amazing brain that is breaking from the fetters of a limbic system hundreds of millions of years old. We just have to take responsibility and embrace our PFC and the remarkable promise it inspires.

Our ability to show admiration and gratitude is as deeply a part of us as the ability to show disdain and disgust. Which direction we choose is within our PFC control, and our prosocial or antisocial expression toward another person will influence his or her brain's response to us. We can continue to practice anger-inducing behaviors (and at least know why we have created an environment of anger), or we can choose to do something different: to trade thanks, express gratitude, acknowledge value, and expand our in-group along with access to all the resources, residence, and relationships it implicitly contains.

Exercise: Review Your R's

Go back to your lists of resources, residence, and relationships. Rather than feel envy or suspicion toward others, think about people to whom you can be grateful for helping provide each of the 3R's. Consider contacting them over the next few days and just letting them know how grateful you are.

In some ways, human nature really is quite simple. When we are thanked and our altruistic deed has been acknowledged, we feel respected and valued. When we are not thanked, we can feel disrespected and unvalued. Receiving gratitude enhances our ability to trust in the person with whom we shared. Our altruism creates a probability that the other person will reciprocate in the future with an altruistic act toward us. So trading thanks increases the chance that both of us will be more successful. This open exchange is the complete antithesis to a relationship built around the angry feelings of mistrust, envy, and suspicion, and all it takes is a simple communication of thanks, which on a fundamental level is an expression of respect.

R.E.S.P.E.C.T.

In this book, we've explored the seven steps to outsmarting anger. In step one, Recognize Rage, you learned how anger is built in to our brains and how to identify it in yourself. In steps two and three, Envision Envy and Sense Suspicion, we explored some of the key anger triggers that affect other people and how to counter those triggers. In steps four and five, Project Peace and Engage Empathy, we moved from identifying anger to proactively intercepting it in others. Finally, in step six, Communicate Clearly, and step seven, Trade Thanks, we focused on how basic practices of human interaction can reduce anger in all of our relationships. These seven steps are easy to remember through the acronym they spell. Let's put the seven steps together:

Recognize Rage	**R**
Envision Envy	**E**
Sense Suspicion	**S**
Project Peace	**P**
Engage Empathy	**E**
Communicate Clearly	**C**
Trade Thanks	**T**

"Respect" is more than a great song by Aretha Franklin; it is the fundamental essence of this book, and each step paves the way in which you can outsmart the anger that emerges in everyday life. Each of us can use these steps to blaze a path through the woods that, if traveled enough, can become a clear trail for others to follow. These seven steps result in the ultimate acknowledgment of value in another human being. As we have seen, disrespect leads to devaluation, then mistrust and a significant inhibition of our potential strengths and contributions. None of us likes being disrespected, so we get angry and want the other person to change. But if I am doing this, everyone is doing it.

In the chapters on envy and suspicion, we talked about what makes you feel angry, and noted that if those things make you feel that way, chances are they make other people feel that way. Certain anger triggers like envy and suspicion are fairly universal, and they all come down to the perception of being disrespected, which leads to feeling devalued, mistrustful, and angry. We want the other person to change what she is doing. Instead of unleashing unlimited potential, we become defensive of what we have, or try to take what someone else has. This approach serves to activate the same response in the other person, as she begins to feel disrespected, devalued, and mistrustful, having to shore up her own defenses.

If you are seen as a person without value, you are at higher risk of being kicked out of the in-group and having to fare on your own in a world of potential predators. What a way to live—anxious, angry, limbic. How can you learn anything or enjoy life if all you can do is simply survive? But there is no way that a limbic brain, believing it is about to be attacked, can do anything else. Cortisol courses, blood flow shifts, the body readies for fight or flight or is frozen into a self-imposed paralysis of terror. And these days it is rarely a physical threat that prompts such a total brain-body reaction. From your own experience, think how easily it is to feel disrespected and outside the group. Just a few words can do it: "Shut up," "You can't do that," "You can't have any," "Get out," or "What you looking at?"

Anger is a powerful part of our human nature and has enormous survival implications. Our anger has an immense potential for destruction but also for productivity. It has helped us survive as a species, but can turn us against each other when we lump people into in-groups and out-groups because our limbic brain fears a sudden lack of the 3R's. But when you outsmart anger, you see that we are not all so different, that we all share the same basic goal of being valued, and that human potential itself, if allowed to emerge through the path of respect, value, and trust, is a truly unlimited resource.

Back in Chapter Five, I asked this same question: When do you get angry with someone who is treating you with respect? My answer then is the same as it is now: You don't. We get angry when we want someone to do something different—to stop doing what he is doing or to start doing what he is not. But respect says, "I value you as a fellow human being." Respect feels great, and why would we want to change that? I believe this principle has the same reliability as gravity: apples do not fall up, and the brain does not activate anger when it perceives it is being respected. This remarkably consistent and fundamental response includes the social neural networks, mirror neurons, and our deep evolutionary impetus to be social and thrive. Respect becomes the great modulator of anger, our most dangerous emotion. Being able to respect one another for our differences completes the shift from our limbic envies and suspicions to the logical recognition that the more people we have in our group, the more people feel respected and valued, the more access we have to their resources, residence, and relationships. Respect is a fundamental tool for success.

How does it ever make survival sense to expend your own energy preparing to use fight, fight, or freeze to defend against a potential competitor, when you have the fourth F of friendship available? Friendship can free all parties to cooperate and integrate their values, reaching a new potential. Friendship expands our in-group to one without boundaries, and transforms the perception of limited resources, residence, and relationships for which we must compete to survive into a global residence of unlimited resources, safety, and altruism.

Only through respect and mutual value can we move away from the limbic fight-flight-freeze that protected us in our ancient human past, but now jeopardizes our very future. It is within our grasp to truly embrace what evolution has garnered: a PFC-powered brain that has the capability to rein in our primal instincts and anticipate the future, a future that is extraordinarily influenced by the potential for that fourth F. Let's not waste our potential or the potential of friendship to control those brutal primal influences of anger. Let's expand indefinitely our in-group and enjoy the harvest of all those potential resources, residences, and relationships.

If anger is an emotion designed to change the behavior of others, then *respect is a behavior designed to change the emotion of others.* Respect leads to value, value leads to trust, and trust leads to unleashing our unlimited human potential. You can't control others, but you *can* control your brain, using these seven steps to keep it frontal and not go limbic. You really can use your modern brain to outsmart anger.

References

Introduction

Seitz, R. J., Nickel, J., & Azari, N. P. (2006). Functional modularity of the medial prefrontal cortex: Involvement in human empathy. *Neuropsychology, 20,* 743–751.

Wilkowski, B. M., Robinson, M. D., & Troop-Gordon, W. (2010). How does cognitive control reduce anger and aggression? The role of conflict monitoring and forgiveness processes. *Journal of Personality and Social Psychology, 98,* 830–840.

Chapter 1

Becker, J. C., Tausch, N., & Wagner, U. (2011). Emotional consequences of collective action participation: Differentiating self-directed and outgroup-directed emotions. *Personality and Social Psychology Bulletin, 37,* 1587–1598.

Cabanac, A., & Cabanac, M. (2000). Heart rate response to gentle handling of frog and lizard. *Behavioural Processes, 52*(2–3), 89–95.

Fierro, I., Gómez-Talegón, T., & Alvarez, F. J. (2010). Road-rage in the general population. *Gaceta Sanitaria, 24,* 423–427.

Hunnius, S., de Wit, T. C., Vrins, S., & von Hofsten, C. (2011). Facing threat: Infants' and adults' visual scanning of faces with neutral, happy, sad, angry, and fearful emotional expressions. *Cognition & Emotion, 25,* 193–205.

MacMillan, M., & Gage, P. (2000). *An odd kind of fame: Stories of Phineas Gage.* Cambridge, MA: MIT Press.

Pichon, S., de Gelder, B., & Grèzes, J. (2009). Two different faces of threat. Comparing the neural systems for recognizing fear and anger in dynamic body expressions. *NeuroImage, 47,* 1873–1883.

Roberts, L. D., & Indermaur, D. W. (2008). The "homogamy" of road rage revisited. *Violence and Victims, 23,* 758–772.

Sansone, R. A., & Sansone, L. A. (2010). Road rage: What's driving it? *Psychiatry* (Edgmont), *7*(7), 14–18.

Seabright, P. (2004). *The company of strangers: A natural history of economic life.* Princeton, NJ: Princeton University Press.

Wilson, E. O. (2012). *The social conquest of Earth.* New York: Liveright, p. 7.

Zhou, X., Vohs, K. D., & Baumeister, R. F. (2009). The symbolic power of money: Reminders of money alter social distress and physical pain. *Psychological Science, 20,* 700–706.

Chapter 2

Braungart-Rieker, J. M., & Stifter, C. A. (1996). Infants' responses to frustrating situations: Continuity and change in reactivity and regulation. *Child Development, 67,* 1767–1779.

Cecchini, M., Lai, C., & Langher, V. (2010). Dysphonic newborn cries allow prediction of their perceived meaning. *Infant Behavior & Development, 33,* 314–320.

DeWall, C. N., Deckman, T., Gailliot, M. T., & Bushman, B. J. (2011). Sweetened blood cools hot tempers: Physiological self-control and aggression. *Aggressive Behavior, 37*(1), 73–80.

Larson, C. L., Aronoff, J., Stearns, J. J. (2007). The shape of threat: Simple geometric forms evoke rapid and sustained capture of attention. *Emotion, 7,* 526–534.

Ohira, T. (2010). Psychological distress and cardiovascular disease: The Circulatory Risk in Communities Study (CIRCS). *Journal of Epidemiology, 20,* 185–191.

Smith, M., Hubbard, J. A., & Laurenceau, J. P. (2011). Profiles of anger control in second-grade children: Examination of self-report, observational, and physiological components. *Journal of Experimental Child Psychology, 110*, 213–226.

Tipples, J. (2011). When time stands still: Fear-specific modulation of temporal bias due to threat. *Emotion, 11*, 74–80.

Watson, D. G., Blagrove, E., & Selwood, S. (2011). Emotional triangles: A test of emotion-based attentional capture by simple geometric shapes. *Cognition & Emotion, 25*, 1149–1164.

Chapter 3

Carter, T. J., & Gilovich, T. (2012). I am what I do, not what I have: The differential centrality of experiential and material purchases to the self. *Journal of Personality and Social Psychology, 102*, 1304–1317.

DeLeire, T., & Kalil, A. (2010). Does consumption buy happiness? Evidence from the United States. *International Review of Economics, 57*, 163–176.

Dvash, J., Gilam, G., Ben-Ze'ev, A., Hendler, T., & Shamay-Tsoory, S. G. (2010). The envious brain: The neural basis of social comparison. *Human Brain Mapping, 31*, 1741–1750.

Feather, N. T. (1989). Attitudes towards the high achiever: The fall of the tall poppy. *Australian Journal of Psychology, 41*, 239–267.

Fiske, S. (2011). *Envy up, scorn down: How status divides us.* New York: Russell Sage Foundation.

Gino, F., & Pierce, L. (2009). Dishonesty in the name of equity. *Psychological Science, 20*, 1153–1160.

Hill, S. E., Delpriore, D. J., & Vaughan, P. W. (2011). The cognitive consequences of envy: Attention, memory, and self-regulatory depletion. *Journal of Personality and Social Psychology, 101*, 653–666.

Rodriguez Mosquera, P. M., Parrott, W. G., & Hurtado de Mendoza, A. (2010). I fear your envy, I rejoice in your coveting: On the ambivalent experience of being envied by others. *Journal of Personality and Social Psychology, 99*, 842–854.

Sue, M.J.E. (1842). *Mathilde: Memoires d'un jeune femme.* Paris: Charles Gosselin.

Takahashi, H., Kato, M., Matsuura, M., Mobbs, D., Suhara, T., & Okubo, Y. (2009). When your gain is my pain and your pain is my gain: Neural correlates of envy and schadenfreude. *Science, 323,* 937–939.

van de Van, N., Zeelenberg, M., & Pieters, R. (2009). Leveling up and down: The experiences of benign and malicious envy. *Emotion, 9,* 419–429.

van de Ven, N., Zeelenberg, M., & Pieters R. (2011). The envy premium in product evaluation. *Journal of Consumer Research, 37,* 984–988.

Chapter 4

Anger as adversary: Anger may help lawyers win in court, but not at home. (1997, May 19). Legal Times. Retrieved from http://compassionpower .com/AngerandthePracticeofLaw.php.

Bar, M., Neta, M., & Linz, H. (2006). Very first impressions. *Emotion, 6,* 269–278.

Gilbert, T., Martin, R., & Coulson, M. (2011). Attentional biases using the body in the crowd task: Are angry body postures detected more rapidly? *Cognition & Emotion, 25,* 700–708.

Haas, B. W., Hoeft, F., Searcy, Y. M., Mills, D., Bellugi, U., & Reiss, A. (2010). Individual differences in social behavior predict amygdala response to fearful facial expressions in Williams syndrome. *Neuropsychologia, 48,* 1283–1288.

Hunnius, S. (2007). The early development of visual attention and its implications for social and cognitive development. *Progress in Brain Research, 164,* 187–209.

Larson, R. C. (1987). Perspectives on queues: Social justice and the psychology of queueing. *Operations Research, 35,* 895–905.

Lemay, E. P., Jr., & Dudley, K. L. (2009). Implications of reflected appraisals of interpersonal insecurity for suspicion and power. *Personality and Social Psychology Bulletin, 35,* 1672–1686.

Meyer-Lindenberg, A., Hariri, A. R., Munoz, K. E., Mervis, C. B., Mattay, V. S., Morris, C. A., and Berman, K. F. (2005). Neural correlates of genetically abnormal social cognition in Williams syndrome. *Nature Neuroscience, 8,* 991–993.

Montague, P. R., & Berns, G. S. (2002). Hyperscanning: Simultaneous fMRI during linked social interactions. *NeuroImage, 16*, 1159–1164.

Moore, S. L., & Wilson, K. (2002). Parasites as a viability cost of sexual selection in natural populations of mammals. *Science, 297*, 2015–2018.

Muise, A., Christofides, E., & Desmarais, S. (2009). More information than you ever wanted: Does Facebook bring out the green-eyed monster of jealousy? *Cyberpsychology & Behavior, 12*, 441–444.

Santos, A., Meyer-Lindenberg, A., & Deruelle, C. (2010). Absence of racial, but not gender, stereotyping in Williams syndrome children. *Current Biology, 20*, R307–308.

Schwarz, K. A., Wieser, M. J., Gerdes, A. B., Mühlberger, A., & Pauli, P. (2012, March 5). Why are you looking like that? How the context influences evaluation and processing of human faces. *Social Cognitive and Affective Neuroscience.* doi: 10.1093/scan/nss013.

Senju, A., & Johnson, M. H. (2009). The eye contact effect: Mechanisms and development. *Trends in Cognitive Sciences, 13*, 127–134.

Tsuchiya, N., Moradi, F., Felsen, C., Yamazaki, M., & Adolphs, R. (2009). Intact rapid detection of fearful faces in the absence of the amygdala. *Nature Neuroscience, 12*, 1224–1225.

Wirth, J. H, Sacco, D. F., Hugenberg, K., & Williams, K. D. (2010). Eye gaze as relational evaluation: Averted eye gaze leads to feelings of ostracism and relational devaluation. *Social Psychology Bulletin, 36*, 869–882.

Chapter 5

Bastiaansen, J. A., Thioux, M., & Keysers, C. (2009). Evidence for mirror systems in emotions. *Philosophical Transactions of the Royal Society of London, Series B: Biological Sciences, 364*, 2391–2404.

Bien, N., Roebroeck, A., Goebel, R., & Sack, A. T. (2009). The brain's intention to imitate: The neurobiology of intentional versus automatic imitation. *Cerebral Cortex, 19*, 2338–2351.

Cattaneo, L., & Rizzolatti, G. (2009). The mirror neuron system. *Archives of Neurology, 66*, 557–560.

Chiao, J. Y., Bowman, N. E., & Gill, H. (2008). The political gender gap: Gender bias in facial inferences that predict voting behavior. *PLoS One*, *3*(10), e3666.

Gallese, V., Fadiga, L., Fogassi, L., & Rizzolatti, G. (1996). Action recognition in the premotor cortex. *Brain*, *119*(Pt 2), 593–609.

Kéri, S., & Kiss, I. (2011). Oxytocin response in a trust game and habituation of arousal. *Physiology and Behavior*, *102*, 221–224.

Menz, M. M., McNamara, A., Klemen, J., & Binkofski, F. (2009). Dissociating networks of imitation. *Human Brain Mapping*, *30*, 3339–3350.

Mikolajczak, M., Gross, J. J., Lane, A., Corneille, O., de Timary, P., & Luminet, O. (2010). Oxytocin makes people trusting, not gullible. *Psychological Science*, *21*, 1072–1074.

Nash, R. A., Bryer, O. M., & Schlaghecken, F. (2010). Look who's talking! Facial appearance can bias source monitoring. *Memory*, *18*, 451–457.

Phillips, K. A., & Menard, W. (2011). Olfactory reference syndrome: Demographic and clinical features of imagined body odor. *General Hospital Psychiatry*, *33*, 398–406.

Ritvo, E., Del Rosso, J. Q., Stillman, M. A., & La Riche, C. (2011). Psychosocial judgements and perceptions of adolescents with acne vulgaris: A blinded, controlled comparison of adult and peer evaluations. *BioPsychoSocial Medicine*, *5*(1), 11.

Shackman, A. J., Maxwell, J. S., McMenamin, B. W., Greischar, L. L., & Davidson, R. J. (2011). Stress potentiates early and attenuates late stages of visual processing. *Journal of Neuroscience*, *31*, 1156–1161.

Todorov, J. (2006). First impressions: Making up your mind after a 100-ms exposure to a face. *Psychological Science*, *17*, 592–598.

Chapter 6

de Waal, F. B. (2008). Putting the altruism back into altruism: The evolution of empathy. *Annual Review of Psychology*, *59*, 279–300.

Kelly, J. F., Hoeppner, B., Stout, R. L., & Pagano, M. (2012). Determining the relative importance of the mechanisms of behavior change within Alcoholics Anonymous: A multiple mediator analysis. *Addiction, 107*, 289–299.

Pepler, D. J., & Craig, W. (1995). A peek behind the fence: Naturalistic observations of aggressive children with remote audiovisual recording. *Developmental Psychology, 31*, 548–553.

Premack, D., & Woodruff, G. (1978). Does the chimpanzee have theory of mind? *Behavioral and Brain Sciences, 1*, 515–526.

Samson, A. C., Lackner, H. K., Weiss, E. M., & Papousek, I. (2011). Perception of other people's mental states affects humor in social anxiety. *Journal of Behavior Therapy and Experimental Psychiatry, 43*, 625–631.

Schonert-Reichl, K., Smith, V., Zaidman-Zait, A., & Hertzman, C. (2003). Impact of the "Roots of Empathy" program on emotional and social competence among elementary school–aged children: Theoretical, developmental, and contextual considerations. Paper presented at Evaluating School-Based Prevention Programs for Emotional and Social Competence: Considering Context, Process, and Cumulative Effects, a symposium of the Society for Research in Child Development (SRCD), Tampa, FL.

Slovic, P. (2007). "If I look at the mass I will never act": Psychic numbing and genocide. *Judgment and Decision Making, 2*, 79–95.

Warneken, F., & Tomasello, M. (2006). Altruistic helping in human infants and young chimpanzees. *Science, 311*, 1301–1303.

Wilson, E. O. (2012). *The social conquest of Earth*. New York: Liveright.

Wimmer, H., & Perner, J. (1983). Beliefs about beliefs: Representation and constraining function of wrong beliefs in young children's understanding of deception. *Cognition, 13*, 103–128.

Chapter 7

Corballis, M. C. (2010). Mirror neurons and the evolution of language. *Brain and Language, 112*(1), 25–35.

de Andrés García, S., González-Bono, E., Sariñana-González, P., Sanchos-Calatayud, M. V., Romero-Martínez, A., & Moya Albiol, L. (2011).

Internal attribution of outcome moderates the cortisol response to a cooperative task in women. *Psicothema, 23,* 196–202.

Enrici, I., Adenzato, M., Cappa, S., Bara, B. G., & Tettamanti, M. (2011). Intention processing in communication: A common brain network for language and gestures. *Journal of Cognitive Neuroscience, 23,* 2415–2431.

Graber, E. C., Laurenceau, J. P., Miga, E., Chango, J., & Coan, J. (2011). Conflict and love: Predicting newlywed marital outcomes from two interaction contexts. *Journal of Family Psychology, 25,* 541–550.

Grossmann, T., Oberecker, R., Koch, S. P., & Friederici, A. D. (2010). The developmental origins of voice processing in the human brain. *Neuron, 65,* 852–858.

Harinck, F., & van Kleef, G. A. (2012, January 27). Be hard on the interests and soft on the values: Conflict issue moderates the effects of anger in negotiations. *British Journal of Social Psychology.* doi: 10.1111/j.2044-8309.2011.02089.x.

Liu, T., Pinheiro, A. P., Deng, G., Nestor, P. G., McCarley, R. W., & Niznikiewicz, M. A. (2012). Electrophysiological insights into processing nonverbal emotional vocalizations. *Neuroreport, 23,* 108–112.

Nagy, E., Liotti, M., Brown, S., Waiter, G., Bromiley, A., Trevarthen, C., & Bardos, G. (2010, September 24). The neural mechanisms of reciprocal communication. *Brain Research, 1353,* 159–167.

Rigoulot, S., & Pell, M. D. (2012). Seeing emotion with your ears: Emotional prosody implicitly guides visual attention to faces. *PLoS One, 7*(1), e30740.

Schjoedt, U., Stødkilde-Jørgensen, H., Geertz, A. W., Lund, T. E., & Roepstorff, A. (2011). The power of charisma—perceived charisma inhibits the frontal executive network of believers in intercessory prayer. *Social Cognitive and Affective Neuroscience, 6,* 119–127.

Sluzki, C. E. (2010). The pathway between conflict and reconciliation: Coexistence as an evolutionary process. *Transcultural Psychiatry, 47,* 55–69.

Tausch, N., Becker, J. C., Spears, R., Christ, O., Saab, R., Singh, P., & Siddiqui, R. N. (2011). Explaining radical group behavior: Developing emotion and efficacy routes to normative and nonnormative collective action. *Journal of Personality and Social Psychology, 101,* 129–148.

van Dijk, E., van Kleef, G. A., Steinel, W., & van Beest, I. (2008). A social functional approach to emotions in bargaining: When communicating anger pays and when it backfires. *Journal of Personality and Social Psychology, 94,* 600–614.

Weiss, J., Donigian, A., & Hughes, J. (2010). Extreme negotiations. *Harvard Business Review, 88*(11), 66–75, 149.

Chapter 8

Algoe, S., Haidt, J., & Gable, S. (2008). Beyond reciprocity: Gratitude and relationships in everyday life. *Emotion, 8,* 425–429.

Bartlett, M. Y., Condon, P., Cruz, J., Baumann, J., & Desteno, D. (2012). Gratitude: Prompting behaviours that build relationships. *Cognition & Emotion, 26,* 2–13.

Bastian, B., Laham, S. M., Wilson, S., Haslam, N., & Koval, P. (2011). Blaming, praising, and protecting our humanity: The implications of everyday dehumanization for judgments of moral status. *British Journal of Social Psychology, 50,* 469–483.

Bird, J. M., & Markle, R. S. (2012). Subjective well-being in school environments: Promoting positive youth development through evidence-based assessment and intervention. *American Journal of Orthopsychiatry, 82,* 61–66.

DeSteno, D., Bartlett, M. Y., Baumann, J., Williams, L. A., & Dickens, L. (2010). Gratitude as moral sentiment: Emotion-guided cooperation in economic exchange. *Emotion, 10,* 289–293.

Emmons, R. A., & McCullough, M. E. (2003). Counting blessings versus burdens: An experimental investigation of gratitude and subjective well-being in daily life. *Journal of Personality and Social Psychology, 84,* 377–389.

Fisk, G. M., & Neville, L. B. (2011). Effects of customer entitlement on service workers' physical and psychological well-being: A study of waitstaff employees. *Journal of Occupational Health Psychology, 16,* 391–405.

Grant, A. M., & Gino, F. (2010). A little thanks goes a long way: Explaining why gratitude expressions motivate prosocial behavior. *Journal of Personality and Social Psychology, 98,* 946–955.

James, W. (1981). *The principles of psychology.* Cambridge, MA: Harvard University Press, p. 313. (Original work published 1890)

Kashdan, T. B., Mishra, A., Breen, W. E., & Froh, J. J. (2009). Gender differences in gratitude: Examining appraisals, narratives, the willingness to express emotions, and changes in psychological needs. *Journal of Personality, 77,* 691–730.

Lambert, N. M., Clark, M. S., Durtschi, J., Fincham, F. D., & Graham, S. M. (2010). Benefits of expressing gratitude: Expressing gratitude to a partner changes one's view of the relationship. *Psychological Science, 21,* 574–580.

Lambert, N. M., & Fincham, F. D. (2011). Expressing gratitude to a partner leads to more relationship maintenance behavior. *Emotion, 11,* 52–60.

Lavner, J. A., & Bradbury, T. N. (2012). Why do even satisfied newlyweds eventually go on to divorce? *Journal of Family Psychology, 26,* 1–10.

Li, D., Zhang, W., Li, X., Li, N., & Ye, B. (2012). Gratitude and suicidal ideation and suicide attempts among Chinese adolescents: Direct, mediated, and moderated effects. *Journal of Adolescence, 35,* 55–66.

Osborne, D., Smith, H. J., & Huo, Y. J. (2012). More than a feeling: Discrete emotions mediate the relationship between relative deprivation and reactions to workplace furloughs. *Personality and Social Psychology Bulletin, 38,* 628–641.

About the Authors

Joseph Shrand, MD, is an instructor of psychiatry at Harvard Medical School, and the medical director of CASTLE (Clean and Sober Teens Living Empowered), an intervention unit for at-risk teens that is part of the highly respected High Point Treatment Center in Brockton, Massachusetts. Dr. Shrand is triple board certified in adult psychiatry and child and adolescent psychiatry, and is a diplomate of the American Board of Addiction Medicine.

Shrand also teaches psychiatry residents-in-training as a member of the Brockton VA staff. He has been an assistant child psychiatrist on the medical staff of Massachusetts General Hospital, served as medical director of the child and adolescent outpatient program at McLean Hospital, and was until recently the medical director of the Adult Inpatient Psychiatric Unit for High Point Treatment Center in Plymouth. He also serves on various boards involved in national mental health issues and is the coauthor (with Leigh Devine) of *Manage Your Stress: Overcoming Stress in the Modern World.*

Among colleagues and staff, Shrand is affectionately called "Doctor Joe," as he was "Joe" in the original children's cast of the PBS series *ZOOM.*

Leigh Devine, MS, is a journalist and award-winning television producer specializing in health education. She is the coauthor, with

Dr. Shrand, of *Manage Your Stress.* Her articles have appeared in *Emmy, Television Week,* and the *Wall Street Journal,* among others. She is also a former health producer and reporter for Medical News Network and for Lifetime Medical Television's *This Week in the New England Journal of Medicine.*

About Harvard Health Publications

Harvard Health Publications is the media and publishing division of the Harvard Medical School of Harvard University. Working with partners in the media and publishing industry, Harvard Health Publications publishes information about health and wellness through all types of media: newsletters, reports, books, mobile apps, video, web-based interactive tools, and our websites. For more information, visit http://health.harvard.edu.

Index

Page references followed by *fig* indicate an illustrated figure.